Behavioural Economics for Business

Peter Burow

Behavioural Economics for Business

Published by:
Peter Burow

www.peterburow.com

Proofing by Amanda Banhidi

Desktop Publishing by Wade McFarlane

Behavioural Economics for Business

How the insights of behavioural economics can transform your business.

Acknowledgements

First and foremost I would like to thank Daniel Kahneman and Amos Tversky for their passion and resilience, and for constantly challenging the way we perceive the world and make decisions. More than simply pioneers of behavioural economics research, they have created a language and framework for understanding how it is we come to make the decisions we do. I would also like to commend the universities from which they based their research and who helped pioneer this revolutionary field, namely Stanford University, Princeton, Tel Aviv University and the Hebrew University of Jerusalem.

To the team who co-authored this book, thank you. To Phil Slade, for your infectious passion for behavioural economics and applied research and your determination to see this book through to completion. To Anna Byrne for your clarity, guidance, and perceptive insight that always challenges us to think differently and inspires us to be better people. To Misha Byrne, for your boundless creativity, quick wit, energy, knowledge and commitment to the team. And last, but by no means least, to Zane Harris, for showing us how to practically apply behavioural economic principles to numerous leadership teams and coaching assignments across many industries, and for shepherding our team to achieve great successes personally and corporately.

Together this team has applied behavioural economics in very practical ways to solve some of the current challenges facing leaders at all levels of an organisation. Whether it be ethical marketing, safety and risk, performance management, high performance teaming, workplace engagement and motivation, or corporate culture, behavioural economics provides a very human perspective that promises to improve decision-making at all levels of society. One of the ways to inherently counter cognitive bias is by encouraging diversity - of culture, age and subject matter experts (SMEs). Our team of collaborators are a living example of this diversity and include a SMEs in Psychology, Behavioural Economics (Phil), Neuroscience (Misha), Law (Anna), Human Resources and leadership (Zane).

Thanks also to Phil and Anna for leading the Ethical Marketing charge, which is an exciting and current application of behavioural economics in business, and to Zane who is leading the charge on performance management through the lens of behavioural economics. Thank you to Susan Nixon for her work on codifying the meta-study of cognitive bias and for your constant support throughout the years. Thanks also to Wade McFarlane for the book design and layout, to Kiryl Lysenka for the front cover design, and Amanda Banhidi for editing and proofing.

Finally, I'd like to thank the thousands of behavioural economic enthusiasts around the world who are earnestly seeking ways to improve decision-making at all levels of society. By helping people to apply the insights of behavioural economics to practical decisions, people will make better decisions every day, and that will ultimately change the world.

Contents

Foreword

by Uwe Dulleck

Behavioural Economics is likely to be the school of economic thought of the last 30 years that has had the most profound impact on research, government and business. Where generations of academics and practitioners have worked assuming that people, whether they are customers, employees, managers, judges, financial advisors, to name just few examples, are highly rational individuals, a set of ingeniously conceived experiments have revealed that people are far from rational. More importantly, the research shows that behaviour deviates systematically from purely rational behaviour. Peter Burow and his team of co-authors concisely introduce the reader to this school of thought and maybe more importantly deliver insights relevant to business. Behavioural Economics for Business is designed more for the practitioner than the researcher, providing insights and developing them into relevant approaches for marketing, human resource management, workplace health and safety as well as governance and leadership.

In the 1990s I attended, as a PhD student, a lecture by Daniel Kahneman. At that time Kahneman and his collaborator of many years, Amos Tversky, had, as Psychologists, succeeded to challenge almost all assumptions economists, and for that matter most of the academic business fraternity, cherished. Tversky and Kahneman showed, with a multitude of seemingly simple experiments, that people are far from perfect rational decision-makers.

In this book Phil Slade shows us that cognitive biases are not just mistakes but have a role to play in allowing us to function in the complex world we live in. Peter Burow and Phil Slade then discuss several of the main insights from this research on how we reason. Building on the work by Richard Thaler and Cass Sunstein, Burow and Misha Byrne then provide a method for how these insights can be used to evaluate whether a marketing campaign is ethical, i.e. helps people to make better decisions or abuses cognitive biases for – very often only – short term gain. Burow, Slade, Byrne and Zane Harris then move on to reconsider performance managers, reviewing Kahneman and Tversky's research to enable managers to provide feedback that allows employees to reach their potential. Burow, Slade and Harris then take this lens to identify major weaknesses in workplace health and safety policies, so frequently observed in business, that simply ignore the fact that more rules may not be better if a decision-maker is not perfectly rational. Burow and Anna Byrne then addresses the questions of modern management using behavioural economics: what is the best way to make decisions in teams and how to lead organisations.

Many ideas put forward in this book are highly relevant to business and they are a very good example of how we can make use of current research in behavioural economics in the business environment. Naturally, the researcher in me sees lots for areas where further research is needed - but any type of good research needs to start with an idea and its implementation. If one can learn from Kahneman and Tversky's research approach it is that we should look at the data to improve our understanding about the complexities of making decisions, whether it is about abstract choices or the choices we make running a business. Other examples of areas that behavioural economics research is currently impacting include:

- companies, government departments and non-profit organisations as they start to embrace Behavioural Economics to enable their clients to make better decisions, inform product development and therefore provide better value to the end user (the ethical marketing assessment tool developed by Peter and his team currently being used in many industries and companies around the world is a great example of Behavioural Economics in action.)

• regulators such as governments understand that cognitive biases can be abused to great cost to society and will require that businesses take this into account (in Australia, the Australian Securities and Investments Commission, has started to work with our research group at QUT to inform regulatory policy.)

Using a Behavioural Economic approach entails using the insights provided in this book to take the next step of implementing initiatives and social experiments of your own. These studies will provide solid, objective data that reveals the impact of cognitive bias on strategic decision-making. When designed well, this process is fast and highly informative, and identifies causal links that will lead to concrete results. This book is a great start to this journey.

Peter and his team build on the shoulders of giants to generate insights that will change the way you consider your business. If you enjoy this book and are impressed by what Behavioural Economics can do, I would like to encourage you to look for Kahneman's Thinking fast, and slow and Thaler and Sunstein's Nudge. Both books add detail to many areas that are only touched upon on these pages. The present book gives you an idea where Behavioural Economics matters in the real world.

Dr Uwe Dulleck
Professor
QUT Business School,
Economics and Finance
QuBE Research Lead

Introduction

Behavioural economics takes us beyond intuition and helps us be precise in detecting, understanding, and remedying problems that arise from consumer mistakes.

Erta, Hunt, Iscenko & Brambley (2013)
- Financial Conduct Authority (FCA) in the UK.

What is behavioural economics

The work of Nobel prize-winning psychologists, Daniel Kahneman and Amos Tversky, in the development of behavioural economics has been described as the most important psychological work in the last 100 years. Behavioural economics proposes a framework for analysing why people make irrational decisions, often to the detriment of themselves and others. It is a direct challenge to the more traditional and widely used Expected Utility Theory that has been used by economists for centuries to help predict financial markets and people's choices under risk (Dhami & Al-Nowaihi, 2007). Expected Utility Theory assumes that under circumstances of risk, people will make rational choices based on the expected utility of an item or a situation. Kahneman and Tversky observed that this is not the case in many situations, and proposed that people create 'mental models' or heuristics (mental short cuts or rules of thumb) in order to ease cognitive load and speed up the decision-making process, often resulting in irrational and unpredictable behaviour from an Expected Utility stand-point.

Khaneman and Tversky's 'big idea' was that the human brain seems to have two systems of thinking – a faster, less rational decision-making process based on mental models (referred to as System 1), and secondly a slower, more rational, more cognitively demanding decision-making process based on examination of information (creatively referred to as System 2). Instinctively we would assume that as long as we were accessing our more rational System 2 thinking we would make better decisions, however, the key insight from behavioural economists has been to show the real influence System 1 has on our more rational System 2. This subtle and often blind influence on our perceived rational decision-making process is called cognitive bias.

An example of the true power of cognitive bias can be seen in the study of perception and the simple analysis of optical illusions. In Figure 1, we can see a picture that appears to have non-parallel and curved lines. Even though we know each of the lines are in fact straight, we cannot turn the illusion 'off' and see the lines as anything but curved. This shows the inability for the rational side of our brain to overcome the instinctual biases created by our perceptions, and the powerful influence cognitive biases

Figure 1. Optical illusion where straight lines appear to be curved.

have on our ability to see things as they really are. This conflict of System 1 and System 2 is not only reflected in cognitive studies on perception, but also in the recent clinical psychology literature pioneered by Daniel Siegel.

In his book on the developing mind, Siegel (1999) makes the observation that when people become overly emotional they lose the ability to think rationally and they act in ways to satisfy their emotional impulses, whether that be rage, ecstasy, grief or any other strong emotional impulse. Importantly, he makes the observation that, when under high cognitive load, we are more likely to 'flip our lid' and slip into an emotional decision-making state, making decisions we are likely to regret when the emotion subsides (Siegel, 2010). This aligns with insights from behavioural economists that we show a greater susceptibility to rely on mental heuristics or 'rules of thumb' when experiencing high emotion (Drolet & Luce, 2004; Greene, Morelli, Lowenberg, Nystrom, & Cohen, 2008; Johnson-Laird & Oatley, 1992; Sherman, Lee, Bessenoff, & Frost, 1998). However, there seems to be a major difference in the social science and behavioural economist literature in regard to the degree of control we have over our System 1 thinking.

What are cognitive biases?

Cognitive biases are deep-seated perceptions that everyone has about the world in which we live, work and play. Cognitive biases impact how we think, feel and behave as well as how we interact with other people and our general view of the world. They can influence everything we do from the type of car we buy and the sort of house we live in through to the life partner we choose. They can also impact our work life, influencing every decision we make in whatever role we may fulfil. It doesn't matter if you're a Mail Room Operative or a Chief Executive Officer, the decisions you make in that role, irrespective of how significant they may be, are influenced by your cognitive bias.

The cognitive biases each of us have are developed over many years through regular interaction with our family, friends, clients, colleagues and other reference sources such as the media, politicians and movies. The important thing about cognitive biases is that they cannot be easily changed. What can be altered is the intensity with which we hold them.

This can be reduced or increased by the information others share with us, and how this information is communicated to us. From your point of view, your stakeholders' Core Beliefs fall into two types – anti-positional (disagree with your position) or pro-positional (agree with your position).

Examples of a cognitive bias

The bandwagon effect

If a belief is held by more than 75% of the community, research has shown that the power of this 75% will automatically influence a further 15% of the particular community to adopt the particular Core Belief. This is called the bandwagon effect.

This means that if you are seeking to influence a particular target audience and can successfully align your key messages with a cognitive bias, you will end up with not just 75% support but 90% support because the bandwagon effect will give you an additional 15%.

The bandwagon effect also works in reverse. If core support for the belief falls just one point below the 75% target, support for that belief will lose the 15% bandwagon support. This means support for that belief will rapidly fall from 90% to 74%.

Overconfidence bias

Overconfidence is one of the most robust, pervasive and destructive of all the cognitive biases. It seems to be one of the core drivers behind many lawsuits, strike actions, military campaigns, and stock market bubbles and crashes. In simple terms, it is a bias in which an individual's confidence in a conclusion is greater than the accuracy of the conclusion. For example, in experiments looking at true/false questions, people tend towards 100% confidence in their judgements but are actually only correct 80% of the time. Even when looking at chance (where you have a 50% accuracy rate), people tend to have 80% confidence in their decisions.

Overconfidence has been split into three separate categories:

1.   overconfidence in individual judgements
2.   overconfidence in your own performance relative to others
3.   overconfidence in the certainty of your own beliefs

Overconfidence has important implications for investors and the stock market. For instance, investors tend to be overconfident in their estimates of an asset's value with the information they have at hand (which is often incomplete). This means they are often too willing to trade with others who have more or different information than they do. This helps explain why there is such a high volume of share trading, which is a phenomenon traditional economic theories could never explain.

This also has implications for medical professionals. Oskamp (1965) tested groups of professionals on a multiple-choice diagnosis task in which they made judgements based on a patient case study. Along with their diagnosis, participants gave a confidence rating reflecting the likelihood of their assessment being correct. Interestingly, when only a little information about the patient's case was provided the professionals' accuracy and confidence were almost the same (29% accuracy, 33% confidence).

However, as more information about the patient was revealed, their confidence increased to 53%, but their accuracy did not significantly improve. This experiment demonstrates that more information does not always improve accuracy, but simply having more information available makes the process feel more rigorous, and therefore our confidence in our judgement increases.

It should be noted that, like all biases, overconfidence is not always bad. Overconfidence is linked with self-esteem and increased motivation to achieve goals, and can be a key ingredient in creative innovation, resilience and personal drive. It would seem that overconfidence is essential to survive and thrive, but is also the Achilles heel to rational judgements and decision-making.

Anchoring

The anchoring effect is described as the disproportionate influence that an initially mentioned number has on the perception of value.

In the seminal study by Tversky and Kahneman (1974) American participants estimated the percentage of African countries in the United Nations. However, before they made their judgement the participants were asked whether the actual answer was higher or lower than a 'randomly' generated number they had to consider (arrived at by spinning a wheel of fortune between zero and 100 that was rigged to stop at either 10 or 65).

The average estimates of those who saw 10 was 25%, and those who saw 65 was 45%. The estimates stayed closer to the original number considered, even though that number had no relevance to the question being considered. Almost like a priming effect, any number people are asked to consider as a possible answer to an estimation will produce an anchoring effect – irrespective of the relevance of the numbers to each other.

This type of effect can be seen in many commercial settings. In real estate, estimated valuations for properties are socialised prior to buyers putting in an offer. In retail shops, the sale price is often preceded by the 'original' price. In insurance sales, the highest insurance premium is given before the level of appropriate cover is determined. This effect flies in the face of traditional economic theory, which suggests individuals are able to rationally assess the value of an item simply from the utility the item has to the individual. It is one of the oldest sales tricks in the book, and one that is unlikely to disappear anytime soon.

Loss aversion

Loss aversion is one of the most publicised, and most widely known of the cognitive biases. This is partly because the name intuitively informs you of the functionality of the bias, and partly because marketers often tap into this bias in order to inspire behaviour. The basic premise of loss aversion, as the name implies, is that the pain of a loss is greater than the joy experienced from an equivalent gain.

For instance, if I took $50 away from you, the pain you would most likely experience would be greater than the degree of joy you would feel if I gave you $50. This is the basis of Kahneman and Tversky's Prospect Theory, which suggested an 'S' curve emotional relationship between perceptions of profit and loss (see Figure 2 below). In relation to our $50 scenario, Prospect Theory suggests that I would need to give you $150 in order for you to feel joy equivalent to the converse amount of pain experienced from losing $50. So, in a situation where there is an equal chance of either losing $50 or gaining $90, most people will choose not to lose $50 because the potential pain of the loss is not equivalent to the potential joy of the gain.

Interestingly however, this effect is reversed if you have already experienced a loss. In experiments by Kahneman and Tversky,

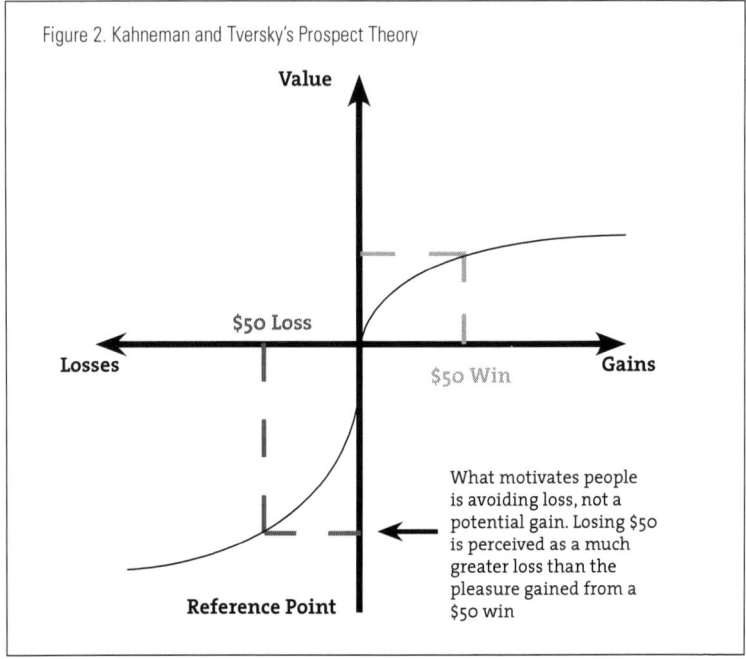

Figure 2. Kahneman and Tversky's Prospect Theory

they found when people had already experienced a loss, they would be more likely to risk losing even more in a small chance of regaining what they had lost. As an example, if you were deciding to play a game where you had a certain percent chance of winning $100, and certain percent chance of losing $50, you would probably need the odds to be 80% in favour of winning in order for you to play. However, if you were unlucky enough to lose this game, you are likely to accept another game where the odds are 90% in favour of losing $50 and only 10% in favour of winning $100. This may seem completely irrational, but once we have already lost, it seems we are much more willing to take a gamble.

Our instinct or fear of loss can be seen readily in negative political campaigning, news and current affairs stories, and social activism and is largely the basis of the insurance industry.

Chapter 1:
Is Cognitive Bias Bad?

by Phil Slade

The path of persuasion is paved with cognitive bias

From the earliest recordings of human history people have been manipulating situations and using powers of persuasion to gain advantage in a 'survival of the fittest' world. Often these persuasive techniques unintentionally tap into unseen influences in our judgements and decisions, called cognitive biases. In recent years cognitive bias (and its manipulation) has received a notorious reputation for its role in poor decision-making and unethical behaviour. However, is the manipulation or utilisation of cognitive bias always a bad thing? Can accessing and leveraging off cognitive bias actually lead to better outcomes? And of course, if there is a line between skilful marketing, and unethical profiteering, where is it and who should be the one determining its position? This article explores these questions, and considers how becoming aware of our own cognitive bias may contribute to us all making better decisions every day.

A revolution in economic thinking

In 2007, the global financial crisis (GFC) fundamentally redefined the way we looked at financial markets and human behaviour more generally. Until that point, economic theory had been largely based on the assumptions of European philosophers and merchant traders from the 1700s, who proposed that human beings make rational value appraisals based simply on the usefulness (utility) of an item to the individual. Utility theory, as it was eventually to be known as, was embraced by economists around the world and underpinned western economies for centuries.

The GFC was a financial tsunami that completely transformed traditional economic theory. The assumption that people are completely rational economic decision-makers was found to be a fallacy. The unawareness of the roles emotion and instinct play in our decision-making was a major oversight, and one that would have devastating repercussions.

The unseen psychological influences on our judgements are called cognitive biases, and if you are a living breathing human being, then you have cognitive biases. This is a point picked up on in the best-selling book Nudge by Richard H. Thaler and Cass R. Sunstein. They argue that when facing an important choice, the operative question is not whether or not to bias someone's decisions, but in which direction you should 'nudge' them. This concept has been embraced in the UK where a 'behavioral insights unit' is employed by the government to develop 'nudges' to make residents healthier, wealthier and safer.

The take-home message here is that whoever is presenting the choices will inevitably bias decisions in one direction or another, irrespective of whether this 'nudge' is intentional or not. In this way, influencing other people's decisions through cognitive bias is not good or bad - it's completely unavoidable. The issue becomes one of ethical manipulation of cognitive bias - which becomes problematic if you are relying on something to 'feel good' as your moral compass.

The reason for this is that one of the great wonders of cognitive bias is that it has the ability to make irrational decisions feel completely rational in the moment you are making the decision. It feels 'right' because it reinforces our beliefs about how we control and make sense of the world around us. The decision we made aligns with our implicit assumptions or 'mental heuristics' that have built up over time, and so we are more likely to trust this decision as being correct. The study of irrational decision-making in economic decisions is the basis for the ground-breaking field of behavioural economics.

Behavioural economics, developed by Amos Tversky and Daniel Kahneman in the 1970s, highlights the pivotal role automatic heuristics and cognitive bias play in our decision-making processes. Their research offered key insights post the GFC that revolutionised markets, governments and economic management globally.

A key element of this field of study has been the close linking of cognitive bias with bad, irrational decision-making. This has had the largely unintentional effect of 'demonising' cognitive bias, and framing it as a key barrier to rational thought. In a way, the pendulum has swung away from 'utilitarian' unawareness of cognitive bias pre GFC, to slight paranoia toward the 'evils' of cognitive bias post GFC.

Through short narratives, this article attempts to show that cognitive bias is neither good nor bad – it just is. We all have our own cognitive biases that influence decisions we make every day. Further to this, we are often manipulating others cognitive bias in order to convince people about our point of view, win competitions, or manipulate situations to our own advantage.

The key insight is to avoid intentionally or unintentionally manipulating others' cognitive biases in order to profiteer from irrational decisions and unfair behaviours, and to become aware of our own cognitive biases in order to make better decisions and promote rational thought.

What is cognitive bias?

Daniel Kahneman and Amos Tversky described the human mind as working with two different systems, simply named System 1 and System 2.

System 1 is a faster system, and is used to describe cognitive processes that are automatic, unconscious and habitual. It acts as a way to conserve cognitive energy for novel and threatening situations. Much like when you ride a bike, you are not consciously thinking about your balance, or about what your hands or legs should be doing. Once these behaviours are learned they become automatic, and free our brains to be able to focus on the road ahead and where danger or novel situations might be. Indeed the only way we can coordinate everything we need to ride a bike is to engage System 1 thinking. The moment we start actively 'thinking' about how to ride a bike, we can start to lose balance and our performance drops dramatically.

System 2 is a slower, rational system and consumes much more cognitive energy and attention than System 1. It is a more conscious system and is what we engage when we need to navigate complex, novel or dangerous situations. For instance, if I asked you to add 1+1, you can quickly and easily rely on your System 1 thinking to seemingly instantly come up with an answer. However, if I asked you to add 249.3 + 94.8 you would need to pause and think about it for a little while before you came up with an answer. Here you are engaging your System 2.

Cognitive bias is simply a term that is used to explain the learned mental patterns that exist in our System 1 thinking system. However, it would be a mistake to think when you are engaging your System 2, that this overrides System 1 thinking. Subconsciously, our System 1 has a large influence on our System 2 thinking. This is why understanding cognitive bias, which is fuelled by our emotions, is so important in understanding why it is we often make decisions that seem irrational to the observer,

Figure 1. Two Systems of Thinking

Two Systems of Thinking

Cognitive bias and how our brains make decisions

How **System 1** and **System 2** work to help you make decisions

'Rational'

- slow, controlled, conscious, cognitively demanding, novel situations

'Emotional'

- fast, automatic, unconscious, high intensity, habitual

1. Input enters brain and the limbic system reacts emotionally, based on existing Core Beliefs – System 1.

   a. If it lines up with past experience (i.e. a similar decision has been made previously and the outcome is familiar) the individual will feel 'comfortable' with the trial decision, which will be embraced and translated into action.

   b. If the situation is not 'out of the ordinary' (or 'novel'), an habitual response is invoked and translates into immediate behaviour.

   c. If the situation is novel, then the information moves to System 2.

2. The trial decision from System 2 is checked by the limbic system:

   a. If it lines up with past experience (i.e. a similar decision has been made previously and the outcome is familiar) the individual will feel 'comfortable' with the trial decision, which will be embraced and translated into action.

   b. If no similar decision has been made previously and the anticipated outcome is unfamiliar, a feeling of discomfort will arise and the trial decision will then be sent back to System 2 for further thought.

3. This moving between the two systems will continue until a balance is reached and both systems are comfortable with the trial decision. Only then will it be translated into behaviour.

   2. Here it is assessed and matched against the individual's conscious worldview and analytical style to reach a decision.

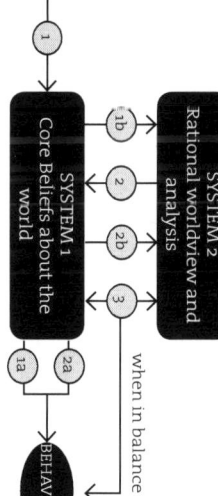

or are not at all in our best interests.

Over the last 10 years, insights from behavioural economics have shown that cognitive biases drive decision-making. In particular, the emotional system of the brain becomes front and centre in economic behaviour whenever:

- the decision relates to primary biological and social needs (e.g. food, safety, inclusion and financial security);
- the decision-maker is under stress; or
- product features seem familiar.

Importantly, behavioural economic research shows the value given to rational (System 2) processes is largely driven by an individual's emotional (System 1) beliefs.

A quick review of the scientific literature has identified more than 170 different cognitive biases, with more being discovered and studied every day. Rather than looking at each bias individually, this article looks at real life scenarios and analyses the role that cognitive bias plays in the decisions being made.

The following stories will hold more meaning for you if you ask yourself these questions:

- Would I react differently in these situations and if so, what would I do?
- Does the character's behaviour in the story resonate with me, or do I find it completely foreign (or frustrating)
- If not myself, do I know someone else that I think might act like this, and how do I relate to them?

Instinct and experiential heuristics

Some of my favourite memories growing up were of sitting in the passenger seat of my father's truck as we headed off to the farm and into town with a full load of wheat after a recent harvest. This was a trip we had done many times over the years, and on one trip I can quite clearly remember my father recalling that he had a sense something was not quite right ahead on the road. He couldn't quite make sense of it, but it just didn't feel right. We slowed down from 100km/h to 80km/h to make sure we had some distance between ourselves and the car in front – a 23-tonne fully loaded grain truck can be hard to stop quickly.

All of a sudden, the caravan three cars in front blew a tyre and veered violently across the road narrowly missing another car as the driver struggled to keep it under control. The traffic screeched to a halt. My father slammed on the breaks and we felt the full thud-thud-thud of the brake system kicking in as the extra momentum of the full load pushed us closer to the car in front. The truck stopped amid a thick smell of brakes and burnt rubber - inches away from a small hatchback that had a very, very clear view of the 'Kenworth' badge in their back window. We are all safe. My father's automatic and irrational instincts to slow down saved the day.

I would argue this is an example of cognitive bias in all its 'survival instinct' glory.

In a similar scenario, Klein and Clinton-Cirocco explored this type of instinctive decision-making in their famous 1985 study, which responded to a peculiar story in the local newspaper. The story interviewed a senior fire fighter who had responded to a 'typical' fire in a New York apartment block. When his team entered the apartment he felt very uneasy, and despite no obvious signs of danger, immediately ordered his team out of the building. Seconds after they exited there was a massive explosion and most of the building collapsed. No doubt, the implicit and seemingly irrational decision by the experienced fire fighter saved the lives of his entire crew.

What was happening here? Based on many interviews and observational experiments, their findings suggested every time someone experiences a situation, their memory creates a picture of what is 'typical'. People with lots of experience in a particular situation can create a very accurate picture, or mental heuristic, of what is typical. Even though inaccessible from declarative memory, the brain with great efficiency seems to automatically compare similar situations with this well developed heuristic. The assumption the brain then makes is that anything that is 'atypical' is dangerous, and should be treated with extreme caution.

Without even realising it, when the senior fire fighter entered that room his memory did an instant comparison with the heuristic of a 'typical' situation that had been built up over time, and alerted him to 'atypical' danger - even though he did not know specifically what that danger was. His instinct was crying out to him "Warning! Atypical situation encountered! Get out!". Whilst the development of mental heuristics over time may be argued as using the rational functions of the brain, his decision in the moment was not based on thinking through the situation rationally. Indeed, if the senior fire fighter had called on another fire fighter to co-assess the situation and come to a rational decision, the consequences may have been dire.

In my father's case, it was his thousands of hours' experience driving and observing 'typical' driver behaviour while towing a heavy trailer. He did not know what it was he was noticing, but whatever the atypical cues were, they were strong enough to alert him to impending danger to be avoided at all costs. The cognitive bias to treat novel or atypical situations with caution triggered a decision to drive cautiously, and in the absence of any direct or quantifiable 'rational' information, it was a very good decision.

One of the recent positive trends in OH&S departments of large organisations is to take this 'avoidance of danger' cognitive bias and use it to design safer environments. Indeed, what it takes to encourage people to make better, safer decisions in potentially dangerous environments is currently the subject of many studies. Businesses understanding and using cognitive bias to create safer work places is a very positive recent development. In this way, cognitive bias is not a bad or good thing, it just is. The recognition and manipulation of that bias is not 'evil' at all, it simply recognises the way humans make decisions and designs systems that reflect that knowledge for positive outcomes.

The loyalty of fuel

Another instance of cognitive bias in everyday decision-making would be to take the example of John James. John is an account manager for a large advertising agency in the city and he is married to Mary - a very precise person who values attention to detail and does not suffer fools. John and Mary are taking a well-earned camping holiday to Fraser Island. Road-trips for the couple have not always been smooth sailing events, as John's attention to detail and rigor in planning are not always up to Mary's exacting standards. John and Mary have always been careful with their spending, and so despite their comfortable financial status, they are on a tight budget for their holiday. Another quirk of John's personality is that once he is 'on a mission' (such as driving to a holiday destination) any barrier or hurdle to achieving that goal in the most efficient way possible will cause him considerable frustration.

Just before they reach the motorway, they pass their local BP service station. John knows the local station well because he has a BP card that allows him to purchase fuel and services from any BP, and then sends him a tidy tax bill at the end of each month. In his early university days the card enabled him to pay for fuel when cash flow was unpredictable. However, nowadays the only benefit is that it keeps his expenditure records simpler when it comes to tax-time. It's a simple enough arrangement that makes his life easier. Unfortunately, the sight of the service station doesn't prompt him to check the fuel level - a very regrettable omission, as it would turn out.

As they enter the on-ramp for the motorway, the fuel warning light and alert sound go off.

Now John is presented with three choices:

1. Exit at the next opportunity and frustratingly circle back to the local BP, risking the ridicule of his wife for not checking something so fundamental?

2. Exit at the next opportunity and use a rival service station that won't accept the fuel card?

3. Take a chance and keep going until he reaches a large BP roadhouse about 30 minutes up the motorway (and say nothing to his wife and hope it all goes well?).

Experiencing an acute stress and cognitive load as he attempts to suppress his level of concern to Mary, as well as increased time pressure with the 'ticking clock' of the fuel gauge, he relies on his 'System 1' to make a decision.

At this moment he has at least two biases that will inform his decision.

*   A pain-avoidance bias which seeks to avoid any pain that might arise from:

    -   confrontation with his wife; or

    -   frustration of a deviation to the planned journey.

*   A short-term bias where the use of the fuel card doesn't feel like he is spending money out of his immediate budget, allowing for more available funds for his holiday (a concept learnt from his Uni days).

With the influence of these cognitive biases, John decides the worst option is actually the best choice. He decides to conceal the situation from his wife and take the chance he will get to the BP 30 minutes down the road without running out of fuel.

This decision seems rational to John because his System 1 naturally searches for the decision that aligns with his biases, and when his actions align with his natural cognitive bias it feels like the right choice. A decision-making process that will back-fire on John when 20 minutes later he runs out of fuel 5km short of the BP service station – a service station whose price of fuel is 5% dearer than anywhere else.

From a behavioural economics perspective, it is interesting to consider the role the fuel card played in this decision.

This fuel card is not a loyalty card. John gets no extra fly-buys, discounts or other commercial incentives for using it, and there is no interest charged on the amount is the account is paid on time. In his early university days, it merely enabled him to pay for fuel when needed even if cash flow was temporarily sparse. However, the only benefit now is that it simplifies his paperwork a little at tax-time, a small benefit that still seems to hold a very strong influence on behaviour. Anything that reduces pain is seen as very desirable by System 1.

This behaviour has also been reinforced by years of avoiding other service stations in order to find a BP, behaviour that is rewarded each month by a hit of dopamine when John receives his fuel activity statement. A touch of Pavlovian conditioning, together with some cognitive bias and we have the makings of a bad decision.

With this in mind, however, it would be hard to argue the role the BP card played in his decision was unethical, it was just good commercial practice. Did it play on John's cognitive bias to benefit BP commercially and disadvantage John both practically and financially in this particular instance? Absolutely. Is it also addressing a functional need that has high utility from John's perspective? Undeniably.

This cannot be said for many loyalty cards and credit schemes that trigger numerous cognitive biases to entice people to spend more than they need in the moment and lock them into high interest loan repayment schemes. Some companies' loyalty schemes span completely different business lines which results in the use of cards to purchase goods more cheaply in one business line (e.g. a supermarket), in order for them to spend more in another area of the business (i.e. a service station). Here we can see it is not the cognitive bias itself that is bad, but the unethical manipulation of bias to disadvantage the consumer, and lack of consumer awareness of the biases that are influencing their decisions.

Cognitive load

As highlighted in Kahneman's book, and reflected in much behavioural science literature, one of the key functions of cognitive bias is to reduce the load on our brain which only has a finite cognitive capacity. The research suggests we are hard-wired to search for simple solutions to problems so we can conserve mental energy for tasks that require more thought. This is a well-known bias to marketing professionals who exploit this trait by advertising with features such as 'with only two click you can be covered for life' or 'buy a house/exercise bike/holiday in three simple steps.'

This bias is also poorly manipulated when crucial details relating to a product are hidden amongst long, complex and confusing terms and conditions. Various companies have been accused of profiteering from unethical manipulation of this cognitive load bias with a court case currently underway in Australia against a large hire car company's insurance product.

The hire car company was accused of misleading customers about how much the customer was liable for in the event of damage to hire cars. The issue was found in the fine print of the terms and conditions, which included charging customers a damage liability fee if their hire car was damaged or stolen – irrespective of whether they were at fault. The hire car company's advertisements would proclaim the insurance premium was capped, but contained exclusions in the terms and conditions which saw some people paying up to five times more than what they understood the cap to be.

Of course, the company defended its practice by stating it was clearly outlined in the terms and conditions, and that an explanation of the customer's full liability was available on their website. While this was all true, you do not have to be an expert in behavioural economics to know people are extremely unlikely to go through the finer detail of multiple car insurance policies to compare and contrast in order to make the best decision - particularly if they are at a busy airport under significant time pressure to get to where they are going. People will take in as much information as they can absorb in any moment, and then once they reach their cognitive capacity will presume that what they see is all there is, and use System 1 heuristics to make a decision.

The reason details are included in lengthy terms and conditions statements is because companies know if they make the product feel too complex up front, then customers won't buy their products. Simply making the products simpler isn't a solution either, because people's needs and situations are diverse, which means the product needs to have a level of complexity and flexibility to be functionally useful to a broad cross-section of consumers.

The constant challenge for the financial institutions is how to get crucial information about their products to customers in a way that doesn't significantly contribute to cognitive load. Having information available on a website or buried in complex terms and conditions is no longer proof of transparency. People can be completely blind to important information when experiencing high cognitive load, and companies that manipulate this bias to create profit are acting unethically.

Much research has been done on cognitive load, which confirms that under high cognitive load we rely much more on our mental heuristics and cognitive biases to make decisions, which as discussed in this article, can lead to poor decision-making. Daniel Kahneman in his book, Thinking, Fast and Slow, describes it as the brain's way of directing its limited attention and processing power to the situations where it is needed most. Daniel Siegel, another prominent psychological author, explains it as 'flipping your lid'. He describes high cognitive load and stress as short-cuts to relying on irrational and instinctive behaviour. What is interesting is that research shows while we need to be under a certain level of cognitive load in order to be engaged and motivated, too much is counter-productive and often leads to accessing poor decision-making processes.

From an organisational perspective, ensuring people at all levels of the organisation are aware of the behavioural implications of high cognitive load is critical in order to get the best outcome for the individual, the organisation, and the customer. Knowledge of the cognitive biases that might be triggered under high cognitive load is a crucial element of:

- high performance teaming
- ethical marketing of products
- effective performance management
- individual motivation
- creative innovation
- successful organisational networks
- effective leadership and communication
- healthy organisational cultures.

Highly stressful and cognitively demanding situations are unavoidable in today's constantly changing business environment. Accurate knowledge of cognitive load and the effective application of this knowledge is crucial to maximising performance and increasing health and well-being.

Unintentional manipulation

Most of us at some point in time have had the experience of being caught short when needing to pay for something at the shops. I have a good friend, Jenny, who describes to me an experience she had recently with a service station attendant.

After filling her car, Jenny joined the long queue at the service station to pay for her fuel with an armful of ice creams intended as bribes for her children in the back seat of the car. It's a public holiday and there is only a single attendant servicing many people who are eager to get back on the road. After some time shuffling in the queue, Jenny impatiently progresses to the front of the line and presents the attendant with her credit card to pay the $107.54 account. The credit card doesn't work. Jenny asks the attendant to try it again. Still no luck. Jenny looks behind her at the sea of frustrated faces, eyes piercing and cursing her credit card incompetence.

In a slight panic Jenny searches her pockets and finds $100 cash. Her other cards are back in the car. She could leave the ice-creams, but she really wants them, and if she steps out of the line she may have to queue up all over again. With a pleading and desperate look she offers the attendant the cash and explains she can go to the car and get another $7.54 and be back in one minute. Jenny gives another pleading look. The attendant looks at the angry mob behind. The tension builds. "Don't worry about it, $100 is fine." Jenny thanks the attendant profusely and slinks out of the shop avoiding eye contact with anyone. She had received the ice creams and some of her fuel for free... was this bad?

Jenny wasn't considering this at the time, but she was

unintentionally, unfairly manipulating the service station attendant's cognitive bias. The only solution to the problem that Jenny gave to the attendant was one where the pressure of the impatient people in the line would increase as she ran outside to retrieve her other cards. Any service quota KPIs the attendant was trying to achieve as part of their job description would also compound the pressure coming from the angry mob. The calculation in the attendant's head was that the extra $7.54 was not worth the added pressure felt from the impatient customers, and the potential barrier to whatever quota they might be working towards.

Was there unethical behaviour? Unintentionally, yes there was. Of course, if Jenny decided this was a good personal business model and targeted under-staffed long-queued service stations on hot public holidays in order to get cheap fuel from service station attendants under pressure, then that would constitute intentional unethical behaviour. However, the fact the manipulation was unintentional doesn't absolve her of responsibility. In a small way, Jenny was profiting through unfair manipulation of the attendant's cognitive bias toward avoiding complication and conflict. This is particularly unfair in light of the fact that most attendants have to make sure their till total matches the value of the transactions. If it doesn't then the difference is deducted from their pay slip. In this sense, the attendant on minimum wage was personally paying for the shortfall.

As an aside, if you still think you are not susceptible to your own cognitive bias, then ask yourself what was the age or sex of the attendant in Jenny's story? As you might guess, nowhere in the story is the age or sex of the attendant mentioned, and your instinctive answer will reveal your own biases.

Looking at the issue of manipulation more broadly, organisations need to look at intentional and unintentional manipulation of markets and target customers in order to identify ethical behaviour. Organisations need to assess their products and ensure they are delivering value in an ethical way while also maximising the marketability of the product. Behavioural economics provides a lens with which to identify cognitive bias and how it is being used, and regulators all around the world are starting to look at ways of applying these principles to identify unfair behaviour toward consumers. However, the conversation needs to be about more than just compliance and box-ticking. Behavioural economics provides the construct through which organisations can have a mature conversation about ethics.

In conclusion

All human interrelationships and communication is saturated with techniques to influence others, and most of them are benign. At a certain point, though, these methods can become unethical, treating people in an unfair manner and potentially profiteering through the exploitation of people's cognitive bias.

We should all be aware of how cognitive bias can influence our decisions in order to make better decisions. There are many situations where cognitive shortcuts are helpful, but there are many situations where undermining rational thought processes leads to poor decision-making. An awareness of the heuristics used in judgements and decision-making allows for an increased understanding of what is actually influencing a customer's decision-making process. It is up to organisations to use this knowledge to deploy techniques that will help people make better decisions about their products and services.

Cognitive bias is not bad, it is just a result of the way our brains have evolved over time to stay alive and cope with the complexity of our environment. Knowledge and awareness of these limitations and processes is the first step towards us all elevating our humanity and making better decisions every day.

References

Camerer, Colin F, Loewenstein, George, & Rabin, Matthew. (2011). *Advances in behavioral economics*: Princeton University Press.

Canli, Turhan, Zhao, Zuo, Desmond, John E, Kang, Eunjoo, Gross, James, & Gabrieli, John DE. (2001). *An fMRI study of personality influences on brain reactivity to emotional stimuli.* Behavioral neuroscience, 115(1), 33.

DellaVigna, Stefano. (2007). *Psychology and economics: Evidence from the field:* National Bureau of Economic Research.

Evans, Jonathan St BT. (2003). *In two minds: dual-process accounts of reasoning. Trends in cognitive sciences,* 7(10), 454-459.

Hogarth, Robin M. (2005). *Deciding analytically or trusting your intuition? The advantages and disadvantages of analytic and intuitive thought. The routines of decision-making,* 67-82.

Kahneman, D, & Tversky, A. (1979). *Prospect Theory: An analysis of decision under risk. Econometrica: Journal of the Econometric Society,* 263-291.

Kahneman, D., Knetsch, J. L., & Thaler, R. H. (1991). *Anomalies: The endowment effect, loss aversion, and status quo bias. The journal of economic perspectives,* 193-206.

Kahneman, Daniel. (2011). *Thinking, Fast and Slow:* Macmillan.

Kokkonen, Marja, & Pulkkinen, Lea. (2001). *Extraversion and neuroticism as antecedents of emotion regulation and dysregulation in adulthood. European Journal of Personality,* 15(6), 407-424.

Klein, G., Calderwood, R., & Clinton-Cirocco, A. (2010). *Rapid decision-making on the fire ground: The original study plus a postscript. Journal of Cognitive Engineering and Decision-making,* 4(3), 186-209.

Obstfeld, Maurice. (1998). *The global capital market: benefactor or menace?: National bureau of economic research.*

Siegel, Daniel J. (1999). *The developing mind* (Vol. 296): Guilford Press New York.

Starmer, Chris. (2000). *Developments in non-expected utility theory: The hunt for a descriptive theory of choice under risk. Journal of economic literature,* 332-382.

Thaler, R. H., & Sunstein, C. R. (2008). Nudge. Yale University Press.

Tversky, Amos, & Kahneman, Daniel. (1974). *Judgement under uncertainty: Heuristics and biases.* Science, 185(4157), 1124-1131.

Tversky, Amos, & Kahneman, Daniel. (1981). *The framing of decisions and the psychology of choice.* Science, 211(4481), 453-458.

Tversky, Amos, & Kahneman, Daniel. (1986). *Rational choice and the framing of decisions. Journal of Business,* S251-S278.

Tversky, Amos, & Kahneman, Daniel. (1992). *Advances in Prospect Theory: Cumulative representation of uncertainty. Journal of Risk and uncertainty,* 5(4), 297-323.

Chapter 2:
Thinking, Fast and Slow

by Peter Burow and Phil Slade

The start of a revolution

Every now and then a body of research is so compelling that it inspires more than just a niche area of research, it creates an entire field of endeavour. The rise and influence of behavioural economics in recent times is an example of such a phenomenon, and is primarily a testament to the work over the last forty years of Daniel Kahneman and his late colleague Amos Tversky. Thinking, Fast and Slow summates this work, and integrates other influential research on judgement and decision-making, which underpins the field of behavioural economics. While the book is an intellectual triumph, the clear goal of the book is to influence 'office water cooler conversations' in order for all of us to make better decisions in our everyday lives.

In light of this goal, there are some main themes drawn from the research that run throughout the book. They are:

- Humans instinctively favour uncritical acceptance of suggestions and exaggerate the likelihood of extreme and improbable events.

- The brain is an efficiency machine. Resisting instinct and activating thought processes draws upon a finite cognitive resource, so the brain will act in ways (usually invisible to our awareness) to reduce cognitive strain, often at the expense of rational thought.

- The WYSIATI principle (what you see is all there is). Our

brain is uncomfortable with randomness and chance and so instinctively searches for causes and reasons for events with salient evidence, often failing to recognise unreliable or missing information.

- Overconfidence and the prominence of causal intuitions. We have excessive overconfidence in what we believe we know, and an inability to fully comprehend our ignorance or the uncertainty of the world around us.

- In this book I summarise how Kahneman describes different cognitive processes in the light of these themes, and his suggestions for making better decisions.

Two systems

Kahneman suggests that the best way to investigate how we make decisions is by considering the brain as two separate thinking systems, System 1 and System 2. System 1 is the more intuitive brain – it operates quickly and effortlessly with no sense of voluntary control. System 2 is much more rational – it operates more slowly and allocates resources to the more demanding mental tasks. Most of System 1's processes are involuntary, much like blinking when sneezing, and is constantly active in informing System 2. The operations of System 2 are much more subjective, and are associated with agency, concentration, attention, and planning and behaviour regulation. It is the interplay between these two systems that frames the entire book, and gives rise to the book's title.

All System 2 processes require attention and suffer when focus is shifted away from the task or problem at hand. Furthermore, System 2 has control of resources and will divert attention to the most pressing issues. An example of this is to go for a walk with someone and ask them a difficult question that requires a lot of thought (i.e. 47 x 23 = ?). Invariably you will observe that your friend will stop walking whilst trying to come up with an answer. Kahneman suggests that in this moment System 2 is diverting resources away from the largely System 1 activity of walking in order to maximise the processing power available to the brain. You probably wouldn't see this happen if you asked a question that could be answered by System 1 (such as 2 + 2 = ?), but System 2 is activated whenever System 1 fails to come up with an answer.

Solving complex computations is one thing, but arriving at answers where the salient information is more subjective and less complete allows System 1 to exert influence. Intuitively we would think that when we process information with the more rational System 2, that it is this system that has the final say in the decision. However, System 2 is described as 'the supporting character who believes themselves to be the hero'. It is the human blindness of System 1's influence on System 2 that is a crucial insight, and why the majority of the book is focused on the more hidden System 1 processes.

System 1 is described as the lazy controller. System 1's highest priority is to find the simplest, easiest, most efficient and least painful solution to a problem. Evolutionarily this is quite an advantage when assessing threats, recognising change in the environment and saving effort for the most demanding of tasks. It does this by using heuristics, which are simple procedures to find answers to difficult questions. One common example of a heuristic is question substitution, where a simpler question replaces a more difficult question. For instance, 'How should financial advisors who prey on the elderly be punished?' may get substituted with, 'How much anger do I feel when I think of financial predators?' Often we will answer the second without even noticing the substitution.

The use of heuristics is described as machinery for jumping to conclusions. Jumping to conclusions is efficient if they are likely to be correct, but risky in unfamiliar or high stakes situations. Take the following example: 'Tom moved slowly toward the bank'. Instinctively most people presume the bank refers to a place that holds money, but how do we know this sentence was not referring to a riverbank? As soon as you read the sentence you made a choice, and System 1 is at work when you are unaware of the choice you made.

Some of the characteristics of System 1 taken directly from the book are:

- Generates impressions, feelings and inclinations; when endorsed by System 2 these become beliefs, attitudes and intentions
- Operates automatically and quickly, with little or no effort, and no sense of voluntary control
- Can be programmed by System 2 to mobilise attention when a particular pattern is detected (search)
- Executes skilled responses and generates skilled intuitions, after adequate training
- Creates a coherent pattern of activated ideas in associative memory
- Links a sense of cognitive ease to illusions of truth, pleasant feelings, and reduces vigilance
- Distinguishes the surprising from the normal
- Infers and invents causes and intentions
- Neglects ambiguity and suppresses doubt
- Is biased to believe and conform
- Exaggerates emotional consistency (halo effect)
- Focuses on existing evidence and ignores absent evidence (WYSIATI)
- Generates a limited set of basic assessments
- Represents sets by norms and prototypes, does not integrate
- Matches intensities across scales (e.g. size to loudness)

- Computes more than intended (mental shotgun)
- Sometimes substitutes a more difficult question for a simpler one (heuristics)
- Is more sensitive to changes than to states (Prospect Theory)
- Overweights low probabilities
- Shows diminishing sensitivity to quantity (psychophysics)
- Responds more strongly to losses than to gains (loss aversion)
- Frames decision problems narrowly, in isolation from one another

The great irony of this book is that it creates an imaginary framework to help understand what causes our brain to make bad choices, fundamental to which is the way that we often create illusionary information to create causal inferences.

Kahneman points this out early on in the book and goes to great lengths to explain that there really is not two biologically separate systems in the brain, but that using the concept of two systems is a particularly robust way to explain and understand a host of psychological phenomena.

Cognitive bias
(or why we are terrible statisticians...)

Cognitive bias refers, at a basic level, to the brain's tendency to jump confidently to conclusions after attending to incomplete information. Kahneman suggests there are a few primary reasons for this, including the brain's search for causality, the use of anchors, the availability heuristic, emotion and the presence of stereotypes.

Causality

System 1 instinctively searches for causality, making causal connections even when the connections are illegitimate. Furthermore, people will be overconfident in their assessments, cognitively biasing confidence over doubt and suppressing ambiguity. One of the reasons given for this bias is that sustaining doubt takes more energy than sliding into certainty, and the brain will create incredibly plausible stories to suppress doubt.

This is evidenced when we have trouble understanding probability or in our tendency to see patterns that don't exist (seeing patterns in white noise or emerging trends in randomly generated data). Inevitably, causal explanations of chance events are invariably wrong, but these explanations increase our sense of control and help form a simpler and more coherent view of the world than the data justifies. One way that we jump to conclusions is through the use of anchors.

Anchoring

An anchoring effect is when we consider a particular value for a quantity before estimating that quantity. Powerful anchoring effects are found when people are making decisions about money. Examples of this include hearing about the asking price for a house before deciding how much you would be willing to pay for it, hearing an average donation amount before giving to a charity, or being aware of an 'estimate' at a fine art auction.

Studies looking at anchoring have confirmed that higher anchors will influence people to pay a higher price than if they were primed with a lower anchor before their decision. The central message of priming research is that our thoughts and behaviour are influenced, much more than we know or want, by the environment of the moment.

Availability heuristic

The availability heuristic is the process by which we judge

a thought to be more valid or frequent by the ease at which instances are available to the mind. This effect is most obvious when we are asked to self-rate. For instance, listing six instances of being assertive will make you self-rate as more assertive than if you are asked for 12 instances of being assertive, because the last few in the 12 challenge are hard to access.

The first six instances are much quicker and easier to access, so this feeds into an illusion of assertiveness when we are asked to list fewer instances. People are also less confident in a choice when they are asked to produce more arguments to support it and are less impressed by an item after listing many of its advantages. An interesting addition to this bias is that when people are (or are made to feel) more powerful, they are affected more strongly by ease of retrieval than by the content they receive.

The media often plays a critical role in availability heuristics, particularly with what is referred to as the 'availability cascade'. This is when a small story gains interest in the community, which generates more stories (often about the interest in the story), which generates more community interest and before long the media and public are whipped into a frenzy. Often public policy decisions are made based on an availability heuristic in reaction to this frenzy, often with disregard to more reliable information suggesting alternatives.

Emotion

The use of emotion in decision-making is not laboured in this book, but Kahneman does link it to what he calls an affect heuristic, and it does play a crucial role in risk aversion and Prospect Theory (dealt with later). An affect heuristic is an example of substitution because reliance on an emotion is simpler than thinking about a complex issue.

This substitution happens readily when we are assessing risk.

Fear, aspiration or hope are examples of emotions that can influence a true assessment of risk. Another basic limitation of our mind is the inability to deal with small risks: we either ignore them altogether or give them far too much weight - nothing in between. Kahneman suggests that government policy should protect people from fear, not only from physical dangers.

Stereotypes

To look at the impact of stereotypes, Kahneman includes the following scenario:

Linda is thirty-one years old, single, outspoken and very bright. She majored in Philosophy. As a student, she was deeply concerned with issues of discrimination and social justice and also participated in anti-nuclear demonstrations.

After reading the description, people are asked to rank in order the likelihood that Linda is:

1. An elementary school teacher
2. Active in the feminist movement
3. A bank teller
4. An insurance salesperson
5. A bank teller active in the feminist movement

Intuitively most people answer that (5) is more likely than (3), even though the total number of feminist bank tellers is much smaller then the thousands of bank tellers across America (where most of the research has been conducted). This is a basic error of probability, and even when people are told the real answer, some people are disinclined to accept it and argue that (5) is still more likely. What is being observed in this example is a basic error of representation, and one sin of representativeness is an undue eagerness to predict the incidence of unlikely (low base-rate) events.

There are many thousand more bank tellers than the subset of feminist bank tellers and the probability of Linda's occupation should reflect that. However, our brain disregards this base-rate truth by seeing a representation of a stereotypical feminist in the description and takes that information to be more valid than the harder to accept logic of base-rates.

WYSIATI principle

Closely tied to many of these biases is the WYSIATI (what you see is all there is) principle. In this principle the mind will look at the information at hand and then use heuristics to fill in the knowledge gaps. The worrying thing is that our brain does this without us even realising it, and often at the expense of other disconfirming information that is harder to process. Quite simply the brain often does not recognise absent information and has a biased tendency to confidently rely on learnt heuristics even when there is no basis to do so.

Prospect Theory - Do we really make rational choices?

Probably the most significant impact Kahneman and Tversky have had on the development of behavioural economics is the development of Prospect Theory, at the expense of earlier economic theories that have been around for hundreds of years. Expected Utility Theory was the economists' theory of choice for more than a hundred years, and asserted that all people were rational, selfish, and had unchanging tastes. Prospect Theory recognised serious flaws in economic theory, including:

- People are not rational decision-makers. There is more that influences a decision than their perceived utility in any given moment.

- There are differences between the value of gains and losses (losing $500 does not hold the same utility as gaining $500 - people dislike losing more than they like winning).

- People seem to become risk seeking when all their options are bad, as opposed to being risk averse.
- The absence of a reference point - you need to know the reference state (historical) not just the state of wealth (current).

The addition of an historical reference point in economic modelling and the idea that losses mean more than gains were some of the most influential ideas to be injected into economic theory in hundreds of years.

There are three cognitive (System 1) features at the heart of Prospect Theory that are common to many automatic processes of perception, judgement, and emotion. All seem somewhat intuitive, but until this research they had been overlooked by major economic theories. The features are:

1. Evaluation is relative to a neutral reference point, which is sometimes referred to as an 'adaptation level.' Outcomes above a reference point are gains and below are losses.

2. A principle of diminishing sensitivity applies to both sensory dimensions and the evaluations of the changes of wealth (a feint light is dramatic in a dark room, but undetectable in a light room).

3. Loss aversion. When directly compared or weighed against each other, losses loom larger than gains (threats are worse than opportunities). Therefore, when making decisions in the presence of risk, people will give a heavier weight to potential losses than potential gains.

The importance of the first feature can be explained by simply setting up three bowls on a table, one with ice water, one with room temperature water, and the other with warm water. Imagine then that you put one hand in the bowl of ice water and the other in the warm water for 30 seconds and then put both hands in the room temperature water, each hand would have a very different experience. One hand would find the new water warm and the other would find it cool. For traditional financial models the status quo is the usual reference point, but differing expectations for outcomes, or perceptions of entitlements will set different reference points. Potential losses or gains should be evaluated against these reference points and not the status quo.

The second feature of diminishing sensitivity simply means that the further away something is from the reference point, the less weight it carries in the decision-making process. Therefore, the difference between giving someone $50 and $150 will appear much greater than the difference between $10,050 and $10,150. This becomes more complex when combined with the first feature, where the relative distance between a reference point and an outcome will be different between individuals.

The third feature is probably one of the most important. This means that whilst the diminishing sensitivity holds true for both gains and losses, the weight of the loss is greater than the weight of the gain. Therefore, the potential loss of $100 will be greater than the potential gain of $100. This feature becomes even more pronounced with the 'endowment effect' where the potential loss of an item that is owned raises the value of that item in the sellers' mind to compensate for the loss.

Further to these features there are two insights that are the essence of Prospect Theory.

1. In mixed gambles, where both a gain and a loss are possible, loss aversion causes extremely risk averse choices.

    -   So if you were asked to enter a gamble where you had a 50% chance to lose $100 and a 50% chance to win $200 you would probably be loss averse and reject the gamble

2. In bad choices, where the certainty of a smaller loss is

compared to a larger loss that is merely probable, diminished sensitivity causes risk seeking.

- If you were faced with a situation where you had to choose between the 100% certainty of losing $900, or gamble and have a 90% chance of losing $1000, most people would take the risk-seeking choice. Theory is that the pain of losing $900 or $1000 doesn't differ greatly, so the 10% chance of paying nothing is worth it – even though there is an extremely high probability of losing a further $100.

The pursuit of happiness

Kahneman could have used the last part of the book to examine the philosophical aspects of rationality, however, instead he looked at why we try to make rational decisions at all – to be happy. Happiness research has exploded in the last 20 years and once again Kahneman has been at the forefront of this movement. But rather than look at measurements of current life-satisfaction, Kahneman makes the observation that this requires memory, and so it's how we remember things that becomes important, not what we actually experience. In line with two systems thinking, he suggests that we have two ways of recalling information. The first is the longer process of examining moment to moment experiences during the event that are averaged out over time (experiencing self), as opposed to simply recalling general impressions after the event (the remembering self, which is what the bulk of happiness research relies upon).

What he found was that these two measures of happiness differ in unintuitive ways. What makes the ' two selves' happy is quite different, and they are not equal. It is much more important for the remembering self to be happy rather than the experienced self. Kahneman supports his claims by describing some of the more unusual experiments that he has conducted in this research.

These experiments involve recording moment-to-moment experiences during painful medical procedures, and then how painful the experience was for patients after the procedure. Instinctively you would assume that the quicker the painful procedure lasts, the more favourable the patient would recall the experience – not so. What his experiments reveal is that even though more pain was experienced in the longer procedure, as long as the doctors took the time to end the procedure in a less painful way the patients recalled the event as being less horrible. The main conclusion is that duration is irrelevant to the remembering self - how long an experience lasts. Rather, it retrospectively rates a positive or negative experience by the peak level of pleasure or pain during the experience, and by the way the experience finishes. Kahneman termed these two observations as 'duration neglect' and 'peak-end rule'.

These two quirks of the remembering self are products of the quicker System 1 thinking, and will always trump the more difficult quantitative analysis of total pain and pleasure during an experience. Kahneman then uses these conceptual findings to explain a number of unintuitive observations, such as:

- French mothers spend less time around their children, but enjoy them more;
- Poor people are effected more by headaches;
- Women who live alone record similar levels of well-being to women who live with a partner;
- In early 2000s, in America, a household income of around $75,000 was sufficient to reach a maximum level of happiness.

Conclusion

There is no doubt that Prospect Theory has deficiencies, with major blind spots including the real effects of regret or disappointment on decision-making. However, models that have attempted to include these elements have ended up being much more complex, and fail to arrive at markedly different forecasts than Prospect Theory. The beauty of Kahneman's model lies in its simplicity and applicability. In his words, "Scientists use theories as a bag of working tools, and they will not take on the burden of a heavier bag unless the new tools are very useful."(p288)

One can only wonder if Kahneman ended his book with studies about happiness as a way of applying the 'peak-end' rule. What is in no doubt is that the work by Kahneman and Tversky has revolutionised economic thinking, and the way we conceptualise the decision-making process. This book eloquently summarises this ground-breaking research, and offers many useful tools such as the WYSIATI principle, the two systems of thinking and Prospect Theory, which can be easily applied to everyday decision-making.

Chapter 3: Ethical Marketing

by Peter Burow and Misha Byrne

With the ethics and conduct of the Australian financial planning sector actively under review, many consumers are now questioning the integrity of financial institutions in general. Financial regulators are also now searching for more rigorous frameworks to define ethical practice. In this article, we review the emerging evidence that behavioural economics can help define a balanced view of what constitutes ethical practice in the development and marketing of financial products, grounded in a more informed understanding of the consumer brain.

The rise of ethical marketing

As consumers of financial products, we may like to think that we make decisions rationally most of the time. Sadly, however, evidence from psychological and neuroscientific research demonstrates that this is not the case. Instead, inherent biases in our decision-making can lead to consistently poor choices with far-reaching consequences for the consumer and their financial position.

The field of behavioural economics has been around since the early 1980s but has increased in profile since the global financial crisis, when many financial institutions came under the spotlight for employing questionable sales tactics; the high prevalence of consumers making misguided financial decisions (leading to dire individual and systemic outcomes) became a burning discussion topic around the world. At around the same time, neuroscientists were discovering more about the important role that cognitive bias plays in our decision-making.

In this chapter we examine:

- The rise of ethical marketing.
- How it draws on the insights of behavioural economics.
- Its potential for helping us understand consumer buying decisions.
- Its present influence and application around the globe.
- Its potential impact.

What is behavioural economics?

Behavioural economics takes us beyond intuition and helps us be precise in detecting, understanding, and remedying problems that arise from consumer mistakes.

- Erta, Hunt, Iscenko & Brambley (2013),
UK Financial Conduct Authority (FCA)

It is common for consumers of financial products to make decisions that may not be within their best interests. Yet being able to quantify consumer mistakes has traditionally been problematic. Why do we want to quantify them?

Findings from neuroscience have helped explain why we think and behave the way we do. They have shown, for example, that when making many decisions human beings consistently rely on intuitive, automatic decision-making rules grounded in emotion rather than 'spend the brainpower' on engaging in rational, deliberate thought. Moreover, emotions have been shown to be central to the decision-making process even when we have all the facts and data at hand to make so called 'rational' decisions.

Much of the time, these thought processes take place without significant consequences. Indeed, the many hundreds of 'emotional decisions' we each make are what help us get through life. But what happens when we are faced with important decisions, either private or professional? At these times, especially when we are under pressure (be it from time, a salesman, or financial pressure), the 'cognitive bias' that drives our automatic, emotional responses may lead us to misjudge situations, make mistakes or choose to venture down a path with unwanted outcomes.

Behavioural economics applies this insight to try and understand the financial decisions consumers make. Because the human brain relies on heuristics (experience-based rules) to enable effective real-time decision-making, all purchases we make are subject to bias in one form or another.

The purpose of behavioural economics is to better understand the biases affecting consumers' buying choices, to identify why mistakes are made and to help solve the problems presented by poor choices.

Essentially it seeks to answer these two key questions:

1. Why do so many consumers make 'sub-optimal' decisions when selecting financial products?

2. Why do they sometimes choose products that do not deliver what they are seeking over products that are better suited to their needs?

How valid are the theories?

The work of Nobel prize-winning psychologist Daniel Kahneman and an army of renowned economists provide the basis for the theories of behavioural economics. These were first developed in the early 1980s and, since then, the field of neuroscience has added much to this body of knowledge.

Economists and psychologists have been working together

to establish well-documented, independently-reviewed approaches and replicated insights that are relevant to the finance industry.

An important factor to bear in mind here is that, to a behavioural economist at least, not all cognitive bias is bad. Each of us regularly make good decisions based on emotional or automatic judgements - and at least as often as bad ones. Moreover, in many circumstances throughout our lives, the more emotional a decision is, the more strongly an individual will defend it (and many will - and have - argued that it is the consumer's right to make bad decisions that satisfy them).

Despite this, however, the emerging evidence is clear that biases in decision-making, when intentionally or even accidentally exploited, lead to consistently bad decisions by consumers that tip the playing field well into the seller's advantage with little benefit to the purchaser.

To a behavioural economist, a key question, therefore, has to be asked: Where do we draw the line between effective marketing and 'unfair', or 'unethical' manipulation of consumer decision-making biases?

What is the significance of behavioural economics to financial market regulators?

Some financial institutions have been accused of attempting to exploit the way people make decisions by appealing to their biases primarily by presenting financial products in a way that knowingly leads consumers to a choice that leaves them worse off (than if they had chosen an alternative or competing product).

For this reason, behavioural economics has caught the eye of financial regulators around the world; it seeks to 'demystify' the often deliberately complex presentations of financial products and services that can lead to irrational choices being made (even by so-called 'sophisticated' decision-makers).

The insights from behavioural economics have the potential to help regulators investigate the biases that affect consumers' financial decisions and to test the need for more market regulation to protect them. The integration of behavioural economics into financial regulation paradigms began building momentum in Scandinavia eight years ago. Since then, it has been the focus of intensive research in the US and has become central to the Financial Conduct Authority's (FCA) strategy in the UK, driving the development of both policies and methodologies to assess biases and regulate their impacts.

As the CEO of the FCA, Martin Wheatley, commented:

I believe that using insights from behavioural economics, together with more traditional analysis of competition and market failures, can help the FCA assess problems in financial markets better, choose more appropriate remedies and be a more effective regulator as a result.

The concern for regulators is that market forces alone will not provide the necessary 'checks and balances' to keep the potential for poor decision-making about financial products under control. Unscrupulous financial institutions have profited in the past from the fact that their products are either poorly understood in the first place or have been deliberately designed to appeal to the emotional 'triggers' of potential customers, thereby manipulating the decision-making process in their favour.

Why is cognitive bias more of a problem in financial services than other Industries?

FCA have identified a number of reasons why consumer choice in retail financial products and services is particularly susceptible to misjudgement in comparison to other retail products and services:

Financial products are complex. For most people, financial products are inhibitingly complex, with overwhelmingly detailed variations in features and pricing structures. This is very different from most everyday consumer products, where even uneducated consumers can easily understand both the product they are buying and the price they are paying.

Payoffs are usually over the long-term. It is common for consumers to make decisions based on immediate issues, rather than thinking about their long-term interests, but many financial products are weighted to long-term returns.

Effective decisions require sophisticated risk assessments. Most people lack the skills, practice or intuition to assess risk and uncertainty when making big decisions.

Past mistakes are too far gone for learning. For mum and dad consumers, big financial decisions are usually made under infrequent and exceptional circumstances (e.g. taking out a mortgage, choosing a retirement fund etc.). The consequences of these decisions are often only revealed long after the decision has been made, with little opportunity to learn and correct past decisions.

Emotions take over. Money is inherently emotional, and so triggers our emotional core beliefs leading to decisions that may align more with how we would like things to be rather than how they actually are. Emotions, whether positive (like optimism or excitement) or negative (like stress, anxiety, fear and regret) can bias our decisions, leading us away from logical cost/benefit analyses.

In order to correct or avoid consumer mistakes, financial institutions need to be able to identify the cognitive biases that drive them.

Adapted from Professor of Economics at UQ Berkeley, Stefano DellaVigna's list and classification of biases, the following list categorises ten cognitive biases according to the component of a decision they affect: preferences, beliefs and decision-making processes.

Preferences: Our preferences are influenced by emotions and psychological experiences.

1. **Present bias** e.g. immediate gratification you get when buying something on your credit card the day before payday

2. **Reference dependence and loss aversion** e.g. believing that an insurance add-on to the main product is an affordable purchase because the cost of the base product is much higher

3. **Regret and other emotions** e.g. purchasing an insurance add-on to avoid later regretting that you didn't buy it

Beliefs: Rules of thumb can lead to incorrect beliefs.

4. **Over-confidence** e.g. an extravagant belief in one's ability to pick winning stocks or investments

5. **Over-extrapolation** e.g. inferring from just a few years of investment returns that a product will continue to deliver at the same rate in the long-term

6. **Projection bias** e.g. taking out a loan without considering payment difficulties that may occur in the future

Decision-making: We use decision-making short-cuts when assessing available information.

7. **Framing, salience and limited attention** e.g. overestimating the value of a financial product because it is presented in a way that is particularly attractive to you

8. **Mental accounting and narrow framing** e.g. disregarding the whole investment portfolio and making decisions on an asset-by-asset basis

9. **Decision-making rules of thumb** e.g. an investment may be split equally across all available funds, rather than making a careful allocation decision

10. **Persuasion and social influence** e.g. following financial advice from someone who is likeable, compared to disregarding advice from someone you don't like

DellaVigna's categorisation helps us consider whether or not consumers are making errors when purchasing a financial product.

How do biases affect strategy, competition and other market problems?

Financial institutions play an integral role in shaping consumer choices. Consumer mistakes can arise when an institution chooses a particular product design, marketing or sales process that triggers a consumer's cognitive bias. Institutions can respond to each of the ten biases in different ways.

Because of this, cognitive biases have an impact on competition within the financial market. Cognitive biases let institutions compete in ways that may not be in the consumer's best interest. In their defence, however, it can be said that some institutions may not know that their products are playing to consumer bias and causing problems. From the business' perspective, they are not intentionally playing to consumers' cognitive biases, but are merely responding to observed consumer demand.

The rise of behavioural economics in the Australian regulatory mindset

Behavioural economics is quickly becoming a game changer. Not just for firms, not just for consumers but potentially for the shape of regulation for many years to come.

- Michael Wheatley, CEO of Financial Conduct Authority,
in a speech to ASIC, March 2014.

In Australia, we would predict it is a case of 'when', not 'if', behavioural economics will feature more heavily on the radar.

The Australian Securities and Investments Commission (ASIC), which is responsible for the regulation of financial institutions and market integrity, includes consumer protection as one of its chief mandates. The global financial crisis, which Australia mercifully escaped the worst of, taught us that the traditional reliance of regulatory bodies on people making 'rational' financial decisions is no longer enough; there needs to be more of an understanding of how people really make their financial product choices and how biases can be overcome and decisions improved. This is where behavioural economics comes into its own and why we can expect its influence to start gathering momentum here.

Martin Wheatley of the FCA delivered a speech to ASIC in Sydney earlier this year entitled 'Making Competition King'. The thrust of the speech was about the benefits of incorporating behavioural economics into the financial services market and how, by focusing on the ability of the consumer to make a fair and accurate assessment of the quality of the products and services themselves, it would promote competition. The main question here, as identified by Wheatley, is: How do we use this science to encourage organisations to compete more determinedly on price and product quality?

As this thinking matures in Australia, there will be increasing demand for local organisations to enhance their understanding of behavioural economics in order to meet the new regulations without it adversely affecting their bottom lines. Many will want to pre-empt upcoming regulation by examining and adjusting their own products and services.

There is likely to be increasing engagement between the financial industry and regulatory bodies, in order to balance any regulatory measures between suitable protection of the consumer and avoidance of widespread market disruption.

An ethical approach to managing bias in the context of a financially sustainable commercial organisation

Since the insights of behavioural economics and neuroscience clearly indicate that all our decisions are inherently biased, we propose that an ethical approach to marketing cannot seek simply to 'remove all bias'. Such an approach would be both ineffective and impractical. Instead, the onus on an ethical organisation

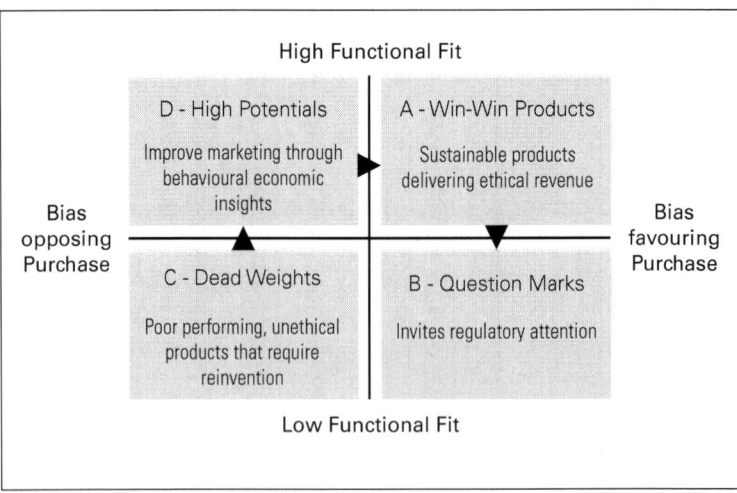

is to consider both the impact of the bias on decision-making (Does the prevalent bias encourage purchase or discourage it?) and the degree of functional fit between the actual product and what the consumer needs (Is the product going to deliver on the consumer's expectations?).

When both these questions are considered, a product and its marketing approach will generally fall into one of four outcomes (as illustrated above):

- **Win-Wins** - Products that provide what the customer functionally wanted and which also tap into implicit consumer biases - typically leading to sustainable revenue.

- **Question marks** - Products that inadvertently or intentionally exploit consumer bias without functionally delivering what they wanted. These will increasingly attract regulator and consumer group focus. The imperative here for the organisation is to either: increase consumer benefit (improvement in product selection support); demonstrate existing value through validated research (validation); or adjust marketing practices to ensure that consumers are purchasing with informed consent and full awareness of what the product does and does not deliver. (Where action is not taken, regulator-led intervention is likely.)

- **Dead Weights** - The risk to a financial organisation is that currently performing products that have poorly-defined functional alignment may become 'dead weights' as a result of externally-mandated controls.

- **High Potentials** - These products may currently be performing below expectations and represent an opportunity for ethical growth through leveraged consumer insight.

Putting ethical marketing into practice

So what do companies need to do to examine their own products and marketing practices in order to satisfy both their own governance and the regulator's spotlight?

Without a clear understanding of the bias involved in its consumers' purchases, organisations will struggle to develop strategies that anticipate future regulatory measures. A significant risk in this situation is the brand damage associated with unexpected investigations that suggest organisational ethics, discipline and consumer commitment.

The FCA in the UK has leveraged behavioural economics to propose three broad steps in the journey:

Step 1: Identify and prioritise risks to consumers

- How can we identify consumer risks caused by biases?
- How can we prioritise these risks?

Step 2: Understand the root causes of problems

- Are consumers choosing reasonably?
- If behavioural bias is at play, what do consumers truly want and need?
- How should we analyse market-wide issues?

Step 3: Design effective interventions

- Are there interventions available that protect consumers?
- Should we intervene and, if so, how?
- How can we assess the impact of interventions?

With these aspects clarified, an ethical organisation becomes more equipped to consider the merits of their products in a way that is transparent for both regulators and consumers, and to adopt appropriate strategies to address genuine problem products and document why others, while impacted by bias, are not working against the interests of their valued consumers.

References

DellaVigna, S. (2009). *Psychology and economics: Evidence from the field.* Journal of Economic Literature, 47 (2), 315-372.

Erta, K., Hunt, S., Iscenko, Z., and Brambley, W. (2013). *Applying behavioural economics at the Financial Conduct Authority.* Financial Conduct Authority: Occasional Paper No. 1.

Evans, Jonathan St BT. (2003). *In two minds: dual-process accounts of reasoning.* Trends in cognitive sciences, 7(10), 454-459.

Kahneman, Daniel. (2011). *Thinking, Fast and Slow:* Macmillan.

Starmer, Chris. (2000). *Developments in non-expected utility theory: The hunt for a descriptive theory of choice under risk.* Journal of economic literature, 332-382.

Tversky, Amos, & Kahneman, Daniel. (1986). *Rational choice and the framing of decisions.* Journal of Business, S251-S278.

Further reading

Burow (2013). *NeuroPower - 3rd Edition.* Blackburn, Victoria: Copernicus Publishing.

Burow (2012). *Core Beliefs: Harnessing the Power.* Milton, Queensland: Burow and Associates.

Burow (2012). *When good teams make bad decisions.* Milton, Queensland: NeuroPower Group.

Sunstein, C. R. (2013). *Simpler: The future of government.* Simon and Schuster.

Chapter 4: From Performance Management to Performance Mindset

by Peter Burow, Phil Slade, Misha Byrne and Zane Harris

Many performance management approaches suffer the same problems as traditional economics; they assume people are rational beings able to respond to performance feedback (information) in a consistent and rational way.

Anyone who has delivered an annual performance review will report that this is far from the reality, with people's reactions varying significantly and often at odds with the feedback they've been given.

In the same way that traditional economics has been challenged by the global financial crisis (GFC), the time has come to challenge the 19th Century 'Newtonian' view of performance management which assumes everyone is just a rational cog in a machine needing an 'adjustment' or a 'tune up' every now and then.

The Behavioural Economics (BE) informed view suggests that far from being a cog, the individual is a member of a complex network or community where emotional issues of belonging, fairness and identity trump rational functionality in the performance equation.

Any good theory is valid until it's proven not to work

Throughout human history there seems to be an observable pattern to the development of new ideas. It starts when someone has a model or philosophy which, through its ability to make sense of how the world works, becomes widely adopted throughout a society or culture. When observations from the real world fail to line up with the predictions of the theory, we write these off as aberrations, unexplained variations or noise. Often, the attractiveness of the simple and explainable is preferable to the messiness of the real world. We don't like changing our perspective and so we stick to what we 'know' rather than seeing the world as it really is. People who challenge the model are seen as radicals and renegades and often even very solid evidence is discounted and discarded.

In some cases, however, the evidence that contradicts the theory becomes so substantial that we are forced to stop and re-evaluate our mental model. It's an uncertain and often uncomfortable process, but eventually the pain of failed outcomes from the old model mounts up until it outweighs the pain of seeking out and adopting a new model.

In 2008, the GFC was a catalyst for this kind of 're-boot' to contemporary economic models, as the market, regulators and commercial organisations were forced to confront tangible evidence that challenged a fundamental assumption: namely, that human beings are inherently 'rational' and will consistently make decisions in their own best interests. This fundamental correction to the model, and the insights that have flowed from it, have significantly shaped our contemporary understanding of human decision-making, with major implications for our ability to predict and manage not just consumer behaviour, but also the behaviour of the employees that make up our organisations and how we interact with them.

Understanding behavioural economics

As consumers, we like to think that we make decisions rationally most of the time and since the 19th Century, traditional economic models had been based on this premise. We buy things that add value to our lives, sell or give away the things that don't. By and large, we choose environments that we find constructive and avoid those that don't. This assumption is encapsulated in the notion of the 'econ' - the idealised consumer who will always make decisions in their own objective best interests based on the information available to them.

Sadly, however, evidence from psychological and neuroscientific research demonstrates that the world is not made up of econs - human beings are far less 'rational'.

Certainly, we have a rational system in our brain, and the ability to 'get our brains around' complex and abstract issues, manage ambiguity and generate novel solutions to problems owes much to the human brain's frontal lobe and its ability to reason using logic and data. However, our rationality is only part of the story, and our rational decision-making sits on top of a highly influential 'emotional' decision-making system that drives as many, if not more aspects of human decision-making.

In the wake of the GFC, it has been behavioural economics (BE) and its ability to explore and understand this less 'rational' side of human behaviour, which has emerged to fill the void left by the failures of classic economic models.

Contrary to traditional economic theory, BE asserts that people are highly influenced by a range of variables other than facts. It argues that our ability to think rationally is affected by the context in which we make decisions and is heavily biased by our mental heuristics (energy saving mental short-cuts that are developed through experience), social dynamics and the salient environmental information available at the time (Kahneman, 2011).

As pioneers in this field, Daniel Kahneman and Amos Tversky argued that human decision-making and behaviour is most accurately and effectively explained by considering the brain as two separate thinking systems, System 1 and System 2.

System 1 is the more intuitive brain – it operates quickly and effortlessly with no sense of voluntary control. System 2 is much more rational – it operates more slowly and allocates resources to the more demanding mental tasks. Most of System 1's processes are involuntary, much like blinking when sneezing, and is constantly active in informing System 2. The operations of System 2 are much more subjective, and are associated with agency, concentration, attention, planning and behaviour regulation. It is the influence of System 1 (emotion) in judgements and decision-making (and the true impact it has on the more rational System 2) that underpins most of the new thinking associated with behavioural economics.

All System 2 (rational) processes require attention and suffer when focus is shifted away from the task or problem at hand. Furthermore, System 2 has control of resources and will divert attention to the most pressing issues. An example of this is to go for a walk with someone and ask them a difficult question that requires a lot of thought (i.e. 47 x 23 = ?). Invariably you will observe that your companion will stop walking whilst trying to come up with an answer. Kahneman suggests that in this moment System 2 is diverting resources away from the largely System 1 activity of walking in order to maximise the processing power available to the brain. You probably wouldn't see this happen if you asked a question that could be answered by System 1 (such as 2 + 2 = ?), but System 2 is activated whenever System 1 fails to come up with an answer.

Findings from BE have helped explain why we think and behave the way we do. They have shown, for example, that when making many decisions human beings consistently rely on intuitive, automatic decision-making rules grounded in emotion rather than 'spend the brainpower' on engaging in rational, deliberate thought. Moreover, emotions have been shown to be central to the decision-making process even when we have all the facts and data at hand to make so called 'rational' decisions.

Much of the time, these thought processes take place without significant consequences. Indeed, the many hundreds of 'emotional decisions' we make each day are what help us get through life. But what happens when we are faced with important decisions, either private or professional? At these times, especially when we are under pressure (be it from time, a salesman, or a boss), the 'cognitive bias' that drives our automatic, emotional responses may lead us to misjudge situations, make mistakes or choose to venture down a path with unwanted outcomes.

The new model underpinning BE has made great inroads into how we understand economic choices, but the same model can be equally applied to a wide range of issues where the rationality of human behaviour - our lack thereof - has led to painful past experiences or unintended consequences.

This includes performance management.

Performance management through the lens of behavioural economics

Just as traditional economics have been based on the assumption of an ideally rational consumer, so too have traditional performance management approaches which have been built on the assumption that employees will consistently and reliably respond to information in a logical way in order to advance their own rational, economic benefit.

In reality, employees are anything but rational when it comes to their career and feedback on their performance. Instead, emotion, habitual responses and bias are all key drivers of the performance dynamic - on the part of both the employee and their leader.

As a result of performance reviews, every employee learns something - but rarely the right thing. The issue of the actual contribution of the performance review worried at least some management experts as far back as 50 years ago. Writing in the July 1959 issue of the Harvard Business Review, Rensis Likert offered this critique of performance appraisal:

"The aim of reviewing the subordinate´s performance is to increase his effectiveness, not to punish him. But apart from those few employees who receive the highest possible ratings, performance review interviews, as a rule, are seriously deflating to the employee´s sense of worth..."

50 years later and little seems to have changed. Today, predictable, regularly occurring emotionally driven biases and reactivity still interfere with the ability of managers to establish effective performance management interactions with their people to establish the right mindsets to drive their performance.

So what should managers be focusing on to drive performance - both at end-of-year and day-to-day?

From the perspective of BE, there are two primary factors, which align to the two systems of the brain. Each of these must be effectively managed to help employees stay in a performance mindset.

1. Functional fit (System 2)

As any management textbook will tell you, any role can be defined by the work to be done - and for that role there is a cognitive mindset (or set of skills) that naturally suit the task. In the context of performance, functional fit describes the extent to which an individual's skills and abilities naturally suit the work to be done. For example, governance and risk roles require an ability to think logically, work with data and project forward to anticipate risks and build stable structures that will stand the test of time. In contrast, marketing strategy typically involves higher degrees of creativity and drive to keep the organisation's offering relevant in the short- and longer-term. Risk requires a control mindset to ensure that people are fully understanding the nature of risk and how it can be leveraged most appropriately. Marketing is a growth mindset focused on differentiation, competitive advantage and opportunism.

For the last 50 years we have been focusing on this aspect of performance management. We have highly developed capability frameworks, skills assessments, leadership profiles, responsibility matrices and job descriptions. An enormous amount of commercial resource has gone into formalising System 2, however, our understanding and ability to manage System 1 cognitive bias has gone relatively unexamined.

2. Cognitive bias (System 1)

There are many System 1 processes (commonly referred to as cognitive biases) which have been ignored but need to be embraced. In this article we highlight three of the major biases, not to infer that they are the only ones at play, but simply to use an example of how these 'unseen' System 1 processes impact performance management.

Problem 1: Cognitive over-load and under-load

However bright your employee, there is a limit to the amount of information that they can process with their rational system - so whatever information is provided to them in a performance review needs to be carefully considered to make sure it has the right impact.

Too often this is done badly, with the employee either

overwhelmed with data, leading to overload, or provided with vague and ambiguous feedback leaving them uncertain of what they are supposed to do differently. In both cases, the brain's emotional System 1 kicks in to try and deal with the confusion, and applies past rules and past assumptions to make meaning of the feedback. In this situation, the employee will revert to established assumptions and past meaning making, rather than learning from and responding to new information.

In contrast, effective performance reviewers capture the essence of the information that's needed and make it understandable to System 1 (emotional system) and System 2 (rational system).

Problem 2: Timeliness of feedback

Another challenge associated with feedback is the timeliness of its delivery. The distance of feedback away from the actual event, has a big impact on meaning and memory. Appraisals of historical events are hugely influenced by more recent events. Kahneman's famous 'peak-end-rule' experiments showed how people will recall painful medical procedures more positively if the procedure ended less painfully, even if that meant that the procedure took longer (which objectively meant more pain was experienced by the patient). In the same way recent events prior to a performance management 'event' can hold immense influence over everyone's recollections of an employee's effectiveness or collegiate behaviour.

When the distance between the action and the feedback is weeks or months, bad working habits form and motivation to change those bad habits is low. The answer lies in shortening the cycle of the feedback. For managers, feedback needs to be considered to be part of an ongoing relationship, not an annual event.

Problem 3: Emotional reactivity

We are herd animals. Even when information is presented objectively, inherent and predictable biases can kick in based on perceived or real threats. Our past experiences (sometimes referred to as defining moments) are driven by a reactive System 1 getting ready to fight, run or comply. Once they kick in, these biases often lead to the feedback recipient learning the wrong lessons and focusing on the wrong things. System 1 is particularly sensitive to issues of reciprocity, inequality aversion and the importance of fairness.

Despite the rugged individualism of 20th Century management philosophy, human beings are social creatures - and so from System 1's perspective both performance and reward are socially, rather than objectively, defined. This means that if an employee feels they have contributed disproportionately to the team success without recognition, they will tend to 'self-regulate' and reduce their efforts to compensate, even if it negatively impacts on the success of the project.

This means that performance management is rarely just about managing individual performance, but also is intrinsically about power and perceptions of fairness.

Not only are we social creatures, System 1 also likes things to stay the same. There is much research across many disciplines highlighting the fact that there is an instinctive human aversion to change. Status quo bias is basically the way that BE explains people's strong resistance to any sort of change unless there is a significant incentive to do so. It is essentially the development of hard to break 'automatic behavioural patterns' resulting from associative learning and repetition (Duhigg, 2012). The key here is that bad habits are learnt the same way as good habits. If better performance is akin to forming better, more productive habits, then the associative learning and repetition is better if it is immediate and able to be simply replicated. The good news is that good habits can be as hard to break as bad habits, but the culture of constantly exploring different and creative ways to do things better in itself can be a habit.

Awareness of our own cognitive biases is helpful. Each of us has an assortment of cognitive biases that are a reflection of a wider emotional disposition. These are borne from a combination of our nature and the way that we were parented. They impact every aspect of our lives. The Emotional Intelligence movement has argued that being aware of your emotional patterns is a key to leadership success.

In the context of performance management, an awareness of these biases is critical. As an employee, your own personal bias can cloud your ability to accurately interpret performance feedback. As a manager, it can cloud your ability to encode performance feedback in a way that will be understood and accepted by the recipient.

Figure 2 (opposite) outlines, at a high level, what leaders can do to adapt their style in order to manage individuals by applying these two axes of performance.

Using a behaviour economics approach to better manage the cognitive bias axis

One of the world's most recognised leaders in the leadership performance space, has developed a very simple and effective method of delivering data in a way that reduces cognitive load, reduces the focus on 'bad news', thereby minimising biased reactions and increases the time cycle/frequency of feedback.

Author of the *Leadership Pipeline* and *Performance Pipeline*, Stephen Drotter outlines a very simple way to have a performance conversation. As shown in Figure 3 below, the model involves drawing a circle which represents the role and all that is needed to be accomplished to effectively execute the role. Lines are drawn within the circle representing the individual performance elements that need to be satisfied in order to fulfill the role. A circle with lines that do not reach end-to-end means that you are performing in some areas but not others, a circle that has lines reaching to the border of the circle indicates competence.

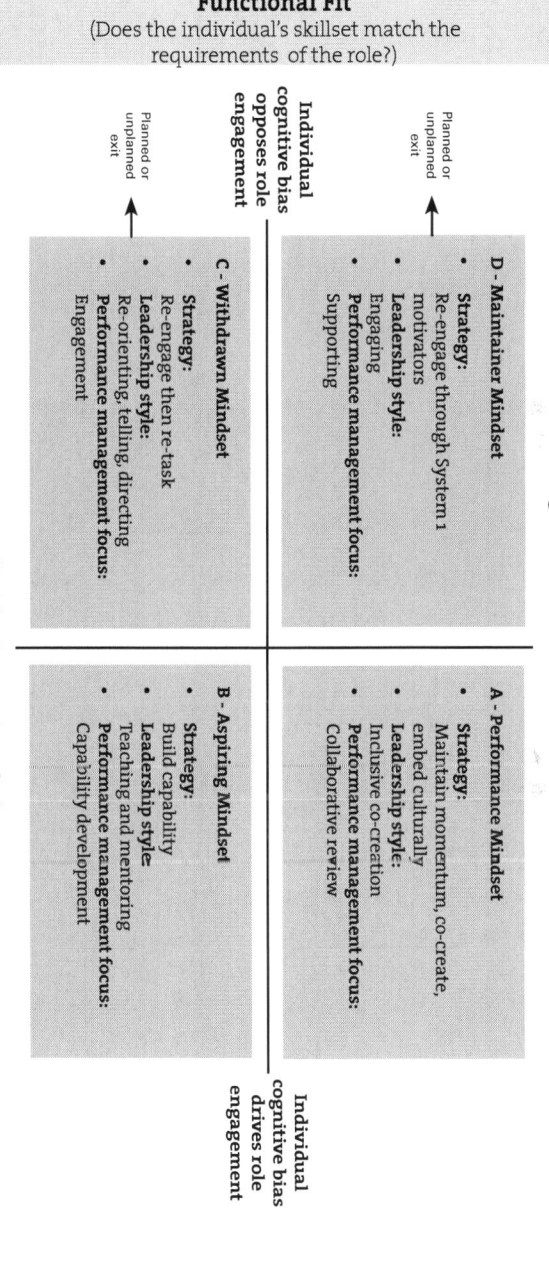

Figure 2 - Individual Performance Matrix

Functional Fit
(Does the individual's skillset match the requirements of the role?)

High Individual Functional Fit

Planned or unplanned exit

A - Performance Mindset
- **Strategy:** Maintain momentum, co-create, embed culturally
- **Leadership style:** Inclusive co-creation
- **Performance management focus:** Collaborative review

Individual cognitive bias drives role engagement

D - Maintainer Mindset
- **Strategy:** Re-engage through System 1 motivators
- **Leadership style:** Engaging
- **Performance management focus:** Supporting

Individual cognitive bias opposes role engagement

Planned or unplanned exit

C - Withdrawn Mindset
- **Strategy:** Re-engage then re-task
- **Leadership style:** Re-orienting, telling, directing
- **Performance management focus:** Engagement

B - Aspiring Mindset
- **Strategy:** Build capability
- **Leadership style** Teaching and mentoring
- **Performance management focus:** Capability development

Low Individual Functional Fit

Cognitive bias
(Does the individual's personal bias encourage them to engage with their work?)

If the lines extend beyond the boundary of the circle this would indicate that an employee is performing above and beyond their role in this particular element.

The circles are easy for System 1 to understand and constructively

Figure 3 - An example of Drotter's Performance Circles

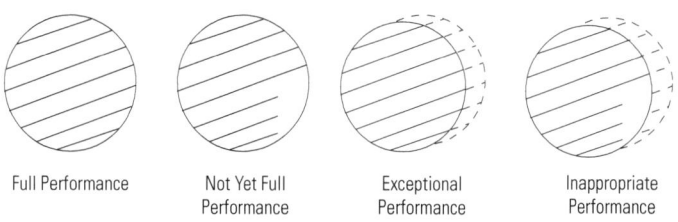

Full Performance   Not Yet Full Performance   Exceptional Performance   Inappropriate Performance

focus System 2 on reducing the lines that extend beyond the circle and increase the lines that fall short.

Drotter recommends that these simple conversations take place regularly to allow an individual to frequently contextualise their performance against the role and allocate their time most appropriately to perform at their best. Drotter's diagrammatic representation of performance has transitioned from a System 2 model of comparing one's performance against that of another team member and ignoring the emotional influences of injustice and other biases, to a system of comparing the individual against the job itself that considers the emotional (System 1) implications. This view helps transition performance management from a traditional Newtonian 'cog'-based model, to a living organism model. This also helps managers transition from a role of deficiency analysis, to that of 'path clearer' to allow hard-working people to perform at their best.

A final thought on performance management

1. Assess individuals for their placement on the individual performance matrix and apply the strategy, leadership

style and performance management style approach to that quadrant.

2. Align individual's skills and mindsets to the requirements of the role - 'functional fit'.

3. Identify your own individual cognitive biases and make sure these are not negatively impacting how you are giving feedback.

4. Actively manage the impacts of cognitive bias on the performance process by following Drotter's performance circles.

The behavioural economics lens calls for a paradigm shift from performance managing (which puts the onus on the manager) to a performance mindset (which shifts the focus to far more distributed responsibility for performance).

It suggests that organisations should start to remove the concept of evaluation events and migrate to performance management being embedded as business-as-usual. With this shift comes a change in the power structure from being a management to subordinate process to being a self-feeding feedback loop (an emotional and systems approach to performance management). In this way, specific performance management conversations become less about discipline and more about coaching and innovation, less about the individual and more about the teams ability to deliver on agreed KPIs.

References

Akerlof, G. A., & Kranton, R. (2010). *Identity economics. The Economists' Voice*, 7(2).

Basar, T., Olsder, G. J., Olsder, G. J., Basar, T., Baser, T., & Olsder, G. J. (1995). *Dynamic non-cooperative game theory* (Vol. 200). London: Academic Press.

Burow, P (2013). *Core Beliefs. Harnessing the Power.* NeuroPower.

Burow, P. (2013). *NeuroPower. Leading with Neuro Intelligence* (Third Ed.). Copernicus Publishing Pty Ltd.

Camerer, C. F. (1997). *Progress in behavioral game theory. The Journal of Economic Perspectives*, 167-188.

Drotter, S. (2011). *The Performance Pipeline: Getting the Right Performance at Every Level of Leadership.* John Wiley & Sons.

Duhigg, C. (2013). *The Power of Habit: Why we do what we do and how to change.* Random House.

Falk, A., & Kosfeld, M. (2006). *The hidden costs of control. The American economic review*, 1611-1630.

Fehr, E., & Gächter, S. (2000). *Fairness and retaliation: The economics of reciprocity.* The journal of economic perspectives, 159-181.

Fehr, E., & Schmidt, K. M. (1999). *A theory of fairness, competition, and cooperation.* Quarterly journal of Economics, 817-868.

Gouldner, A. W. (1960). *The norm of reciprocity: A preliminary statement.* American sociological review, 161-178.

Kahneman, Daniel. (2011). *Thinking, Fast and Slow:* Macmillan.

Kahneman, D, & Tversky, A. (1979). *Prospect Theory: An analysis of decision under risk.* Econometrica: Journal of the Econometric Society, 263-291.

Nowak, M. A., Page, K. M., & Sigmund, K. (2000). *Fairness versus reason in the ultimatum game.* Science, 289 (5485), 1773-1775.

Simon, H. A. (1982). *Models of bounded rationality: Empirically grounded economic reason (Vol. 3).* MIT Press.

Thaler, R. H., & Sunstein, C. R. (2008). *Nudge: Improving decisions about health, wealth, and happiness.* Yale University Press.

Chapter 5:
Safety and Risk

by Peter Burow, Phil Slade and Zane Harris

Accidents will happen in the workplace, people will make errors. Unfortunately, when accidents do happen organisations tend to draw two erroneous conclusions:

1. If people abide by the rules more closely, then people will be safe.

2. If accidents happen it is either because the rules were not followed, or more rules need to be put in place for people to follow.

The assumption underlying these conclusions is that systems are inherently safe - that if we could eliminate any error, we would have a perfectly safe system. This of course is a fallacy. Organisations are imperfect systems, constantly changing and adapting to internal and external forces. Rules and structures cannot adapt quickly enough to these forces, and so the system fails. Therefore, the conclusion is that safety regulations should be based more on principles that promote engagement and individual decision-making, rather than rules that promote compliance and a culture of blame.

When you look at it, these systems themselves are deeply conflicted and imperfect. They always have to meet multiple goals that are in opposition at the same time and always under the pressure of limited resources. It's only people who can hold together such inherent imperfection. It's only people who can create safety in practice at all levels in an organisation. Systems are not basically safe, and we are not custodians of already safe systems.

– Sidney Dekker

However, recent research in behavioural economics also shows us humans can be poor decision-makers, influenced by cognitive biases and automatic belief systems that can lead to irrational judgements. This leads to somewhat of a conundrum – are we to reduce reliance on organisational systems in order to promote engagement and resilience, or increase the effectiveness of systems to reduce the risk of poor human decision-making?

It is the argument of this article that we need both. A higher order of strategic thinking is required to hold both concepts simultaneously. OH&S policy-makers need to understand how the brain works to ensure safety rules and directions are effectively embedded in people's automatic behaviour, and also understand the common cognitive biases that influence human judgements in order to encourage engagement and better decision-making where rules and regulations are no longer effective.

Compliance vs. engagement

It is clear that some rules and compliance-based systems need to be in place to create a baseline of safety. At a point in a company's growth OH&S policies invariably increase, however, this does not necessarily lead to real safety improvements or better outcomes. It is true that as an organisation grows in size, the impact any single rule or process has diminishes. However, it is also possible that as an organisation grows in complexity, people's capacity to keep embedding new processes into their behaviour also diminishes – reducing the effectiveness of the new rule in influencing behaviour and imposing compliance. What happens then is, when safety is compromised, the system designers blame individual non-compliance, and the employees blame the system. No-one takes responsibility for their part in a broken process and improved safety becomes an objective lower priority than defending a particular point of view.

Underlying this problem is, in large complex organisations,

excessive rules and regulations remove the need for people to think about safety. This leads to two major issues:

1. Rule-making as a primary solution. When things do go wrong, people will create more rules to avoid similar scenarios, rather than identify core issues or reasons why the incident occurred in the first place. It also means that as rules and regulations multiply, either remembering the rules becomes more important than thinking and acting safely, or people will disregard the rules altogether and undermine the system.

2. Deferring of responsibility and cultivating a blame culture. With the brain's desire to simplify and avoid complexity (which the brain interprets as pain), people will defer responsibility of safety to the system, rather than seeing themselves as responsible for the safety of themselves and others. This breeds cultures of compliance and blame rather than safety and interdependency.

The blame game

One of the unfortunate side effects of a safety culture built entirely around compliance regulations is the emergence of a blame culture. The problem with a blame culture is that people stop believing they have any control and no-one takes responsibility for their own actions. Employees externalise control onto other people (usually superiors) or onto the system. In modern day knowledge-based economies, employees need to feel empowered in order to be flexible, problem-solve and innovate. If people externalise control they relinquish the power of the individual in any given context, so the best you can hope for is compliance, rather than engagement.

Employees in a compliance-based blame culture defer the responsibility of safety to a process, the process then dictates a way that something needs to be done and therefore you have to follow the process in order to be safe. This is true to a point –

wearing a seatbelt and complying with the road rules will mean you are less likely to have an accident, but a safe driver also has an awareness of the environment, and knows that sometimes you need to break the rules in order to be safe. A system can create a baseline of safe behaviours, but it takes human awareness to be agile enough to adapt to an unpredictable environment.

From a behavioural economics perspective, compliance systems fail to foster a System 2, rational way of thinking, and neither do they foster creativity or awareness. They simply foster System 1 routine-based behaviour, and stimulate a fear of breaking rules, rather than a desire to be safe and solve problems. This does not mean that OH&S processes are bad or that there is no place for rules and regulations, it's just they're only effective to a point.

A process ceiling effect

It is the argument of the authors that at a certain point, OH&S procedures reach a ceiling of effectiveness, and simply making more rules and continuing to preach compliance does not create a safer work environment. When companies reach this point in their growth and maturity, a new way of conceptualising workplace safety is needed, where the responsibility of safety rests more with employees who create a culture of safety, and less with the organisation that enforces a culture of compliance.

This makes intuitive sense to some extent. As a company starts out they usually have a small number of staff filling many jobs in order for the company to function. They have a high awareness of the forces impacting the overall business and the importance of their role in the value chain of the company. Individuals are trusted and empowered to look after the safety of themselves and others as everyone knows each other and there is a shared understanding across the entire group. There a strong feeling of personal control and the consequences of actions are salient. At this point in the maturity of the organisation there is little

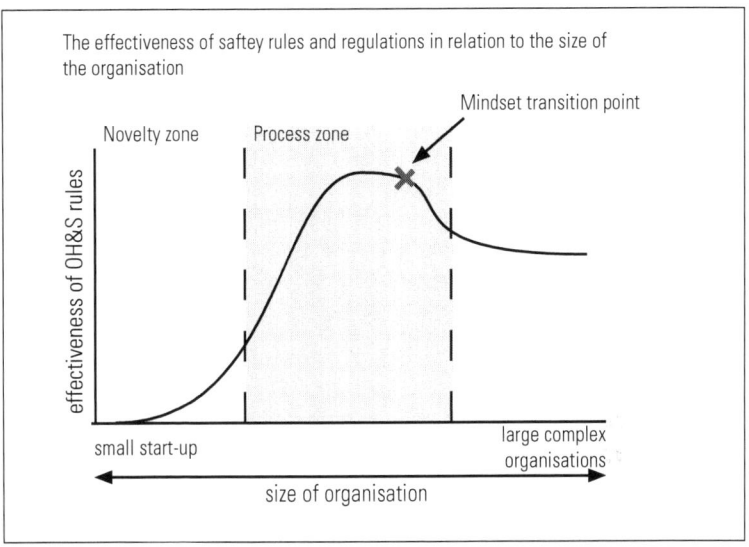

The effectiveness of saftey rules and regulations in relation to the size of the organisation

need for anything but very basic OH&S rules. Employees have a strong sense of individualism and mavericks are applauded as innovators and thought leaders.

As a company grows the focus of control shifts from the individual to the collective group, a greater number of rules and structures needs to be created in order for the company to grow with some sense of cohesion, and the focus shifts from an emphasis on the individual within a team, to a team within an organisation. Processes are put in place and with the rapid growth of the company the processes are relied on to keep a sense of order and reign in the mavericks who can become an OH&S liability as they react to a lost sense of individualism. This is what we call the process zone. Here the emphasis is often surviving in the face of rapid growth, and building stability without suffocating innovation and creative potential.

Eventually, these systems become less effective as the complexity of the organisation grows. This makes sense when you consider that safety regulations and procedures rely on an individual to assess and identify the common dangers, and then stipulate procedures that will avoid unsafe behaviours. Someone has done the pre-thinking for you. However, as the organisation becomes increasingly complex the ability for someone to accurately assess and pre-think common dangers become less likely.

Even if it were possible to identify and create appropriate rules and procedures for every scenario, the sheer number of these rules would make it impossible for anyone to learn and embed all of the exceptions and nuances in order for the safe behaviour to become habitual. Rules and process are only effective when they are simple enough to become embedded in behaviour reasonably quickly. When the organisation reaches a level of complexity it reaches a tipping point where more rules fail to increase safety.

The challenge is that as organisations increase in complexity, they often feel they have only two choices:

1. Create a multitude of processes to cope with the complexity, which then has the effect of strangling the organisation; or

2. Identify simple processes that apply generally but may be less relevant to different parts of the organisation, which can often lead to:

    -   complete disregard of the system due to a perception of irrelevance; or

    -   an increased risk of harm, where strict adherence to a procedure can lead to a decrease in safety.

A third choice is needed, a broader approach to safety, a choice where people are transitioned from a compliance mindset to a safety mindset- a system based on rules to a system based around principles. We believe this third option can be created when applying the principles of behavioural economics.

The lens of behavioural economics

As humans, we like to think we are completely rational beings and that every considered decision we make is without prejudice and impervious to irrational influences. However, we know from behavioural economic research that this is not the case - that humans make irrational and self-harming decisions every day.

Behavioural economics provides us with a framework for examining our decision-making process. This framework suggests that we have two systems of thinking – a faster, more emotional and instinctive thinking, and a slower, more rational way of thinking. The faster instinctive thinking is called System 1, and the slower more rational thinking is called System 2.

Often we use the rational 'System 2' thinking to get our brains around complex and abstract issues, manage ambiguity and generate novel solutions to problems using reason, logic and data. However, our rationality is only part of the story, and our rational decision-making is underpinned by the highly influential 'emotional' decision-making System 1 that drives as many, if not more, aspects of human decision-making than we realise.

Behavioural economics asserts that people are highly influenced by a range of variables other than facts. It argues that our ability to think rationally is affected by the context in which we make decisions and is heavily biased by our mental heuristics (energy saving mental short-cuts that are developed through experience), social dynamics and the salient environmental information available at the time (Kahneman, 2011).

All System 2 processes require attention, and suffer when focus is shifted away from the task or problem at hand. Furthermore, System 2 has control of resources and will divert attention to the most pressing issues. An example of this is to go for a walk with someone and ask them a difficult questions that requires a lot of thought (i.e. 47 x 23 = ?). Invariably you will observe that your friend will stop walking whilst trying to come up with an answer. Kahneman suggests that in this moment System 2 is diverting resources away from the largely System 1 activity of walking in order to maximise the processing power available to the brain. You probably wouldn't see this happen if you asked a question that could be answered by System 1 (such as 2 + 2 = ?), but System 2 is activated whenever System 1 fails to come up with an answer.

Solving complex computations is one thing, but arriving at answers where the salient information is more subjective and less complete allows System 1 to exert influence. Intuitively we would think that when we process information with the more rational System 2, that it is this system that has the final say in the decision. However, System 2 is described as 'the supporting character who believes themselves to be the hero'. It is the human blindness of System 1's influence on System 2 that is a crucial insight, and why the majority of the book is focused on the more hidden System 1 processes.

The new model underpinning BE has made great inroads into how we understand economic choices, but the same model can be equally applied to a wide range of issues where the rationality of human behaviour - our lack thereof - has led to painful past experience or unintended consequences.

This includes occupational health and safety.

Occupational Health and Safety through the lens of behavioural economics

Effective standardised procedures trigger a System 1 response - habitual patterned behaviour - meaning we do not have to think or question behaviour, it just automatically happens. This habitual behaviour can work very well in small, uncomplicated organisations, but the moment increasing complexity results in systems that aren't applicable, people can end up in even more dangerous situations because they slavishly follow a system which may be harmful in a novel context.

The alternative is to strip away some of the systems and encourage a level of System 2 thinking, which encourages awareness, creativity and individual responsibility. It is a change from enforcing safety rules to enforcing safety principles, a transition from compliance to engagement. It is a transition from teaching people what to think, to teaching people how to think.

An example of this can be found in raising children. There is a certain level of dos and don'ts that need to be learnt such as, 'don't cross the road without looking both ways', 'do introduce yourself to guests', 'don't run with scissors', 'do help others who are in need', 'don't talk with your mouth full'. However, there comes a point where life becomes too complex to accurately learn millions of dos and don'ts. In order for children to learn they need to be able to apply principles, not individual rules.

Therefore, if you are wanting children to be respectful of others you can list 1,000 rules to follow when faced with different individuals in different circumstances, or you can simply say 'before you do something, always ask yourself if you are being respectful and courteous to others'. The same principle applies to corporate safety.

When creating a culture of safety principles rather than rules, two processes need to be active:

1. Opportunities for the individual to consciously assess and determine appropriate behaviour;

2. Quick, relevant feedback loops that reinforce appropriate behaviour and discourage unsafe behaviour.

Functional fit

Below is a broad process map of the journey that most organisations go through from basic start-up to large corporation. The key to determining the functional 'best practice' fit in terms of safety processes is to look at the complexity of the organisation and the ability of rules and regulations to effectively manage the environment.

Figure 2 - OH&S Functional Fit based on phases of organisational complexity and maturity

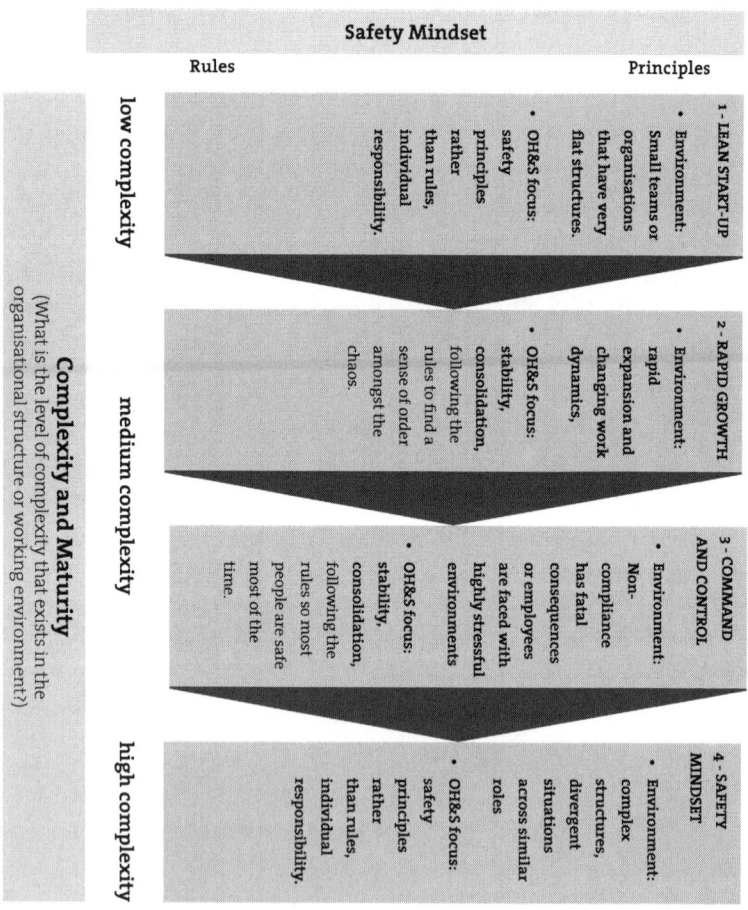

What is important is for companies to accurately assess their level of complexity and maturity and to identify what the functional 'best practice' fit for OH&S processes actually are for them at any given point in time. For a small start-up or organisation with a flat structure it would be a poor fit to have copious rules and regulations. However, for some organisations, a higher level of control may be necessary, and so the balance of rules vs. principles may stay weighted towards rules and habitual behaviours (i.e. air traffic controllers or military). In these cases an understanding of System 1 processes is crucial in making sure that critical safety procedures are embedded in staff's System 1 thinking.

Cognitive bias

Our current argument in this article is that in complex organisations, rules and compliance-based systems have a diminishing effect on safety when applied in excess, and more empowerment of the individual is needed in order to actually improve safety. However, from a behavioural economics perspective this potentially creates a circular argument between two principles.

Principle 1: Systems are not capable of creating safe environments by completely embedding safe action into System 1 (habitual behaviours and automatic processes). Therefore, OH&S processes need to be rolled back to empower individuals to make decisions and take responsibility for their actions.

Principle 2: People have been shown to be poor decision-makers, constantly influenced by System 1 cognitive biases that encourage rational decision-making. Therefore, we need to increase the effectiveness of OH&S systems in order to embed safety rules into System 1 behaviour.

The reality is of course they are both correct. The real insight comes when you realise that this is not a circular argument, but actually leads to a third principle.

Principle 3: When designing systems encouraging safety principles rather than simply rules, an awareness of cognitive bias is needed to ensure appropriate processes are put in place to heal counter bias and enable people to make better decisions about risk.

The key is to strike a balance between rules and principles. A balance between decrees made up of 'dos and don'ts' that encourage System 1 habitual behaviour, and principles made up of questions and processes that engage System 2 rational thinking. The challenge is to design processes and systems when encouraging System 2 thinking that counter common decision-making biases.

There are many System 1 cognitive biases that need to be considered as they influence policy-making decisions and safe behaviours. In this article we highlight three of the major biases, not to infer that they are the only ones at play, but simply to use an example of how these 'unseen' System 1 processes impact occupational health and safety.

Bias 1: Overconfidence

There is immense literature showing humans have excessive overconfidence in what we believe we know, and an inability to fully comprehend our ignorance or the uncertainty of the world around us. This relates to our assessments of our own experiences or the experiences of others when trying to plan the best way forward. The inconvenient truth is that past success is no guarantee of future safety.

However, humans still tend to overestimate the future success of systems that have worked in the past. This common bias is made more obvious when looking at investor behaviour on the stock exchange, where many investors weigh their investment decisions on the basis of past performance. A recent survey by Lloyds of London found the most significant influence on the appraisal of whether a share was a good or bad investment was past performance, even though investors largely knew that past performance wasn't a reliable indicator of future returns. So strong is this effect that even when we are aware of it, we cannot seem to subvert its influence.

The same overconfidence bias applies to OH&S. As organisations grow and environments change, people demonstrate overconfidence in the success of past decisions or actions. This applies as much to policy-making as it does to the practice of safe behaviour.

From a policy perspective, this is where transitioning from a system based on rules to one based on principles. The overconfidence bias assumes the past success of OH&S is a direct result of the rules created. Therefore, to cope with increasing complexity, the most logical answer is to create more rules. When accidents happen the overconfidence bias tells us that it isn't because of the rules that were made, it must have happened because someone broke the rules or there aren't enough rules to bridge the 'safety gaps'. This bias blinds us to accurate appraisals of current systems and practices and overestimates the impact of past processes when planning for the future.

From a personal safety perspective, people tend to be overconfident in their ability to avoid danger. People are less confident about safety when considering others, and more confident about safety when it applies to them personally. People just don't believe they will be the one to get hurt. This also relates to another robust cognitive bias, the availability heuristic

Bias 2: Availability heuristic

One of the key findings of behavioural economics is that people are poor assessors of probability and likelihood. As an example, if you were a skydiver, would you be more likely to die from a skydive, or from randomly falling off the edge of a building? Or, when in America, are you more likely to die from an airline accident or crossing the street? According to the National Safety Council's annual rankings of the top causes of death, the answers are that you are six times more likely to die from randomly falling from a building than a sky diving accident, and 40,000 times more likely to die from crossing the street than in an airline accident.

The reason this seems unintuitive, or at least the magnitude of the difference seems wrong, is because when someone dies from a failed parachute it usually hits the news and social media, however, a random fall from a building receives much less airtime. Because we are more exposed to media stories of death from what we perceive to be risky pursuits, memories of these events are much easier to recall. The ease or availability of memories is misinterpreted by the brain as a greater likelihood and we make an incorrect judgement regarding probability.

This inability to compute probability also makes us very poor assessors of risk. This is not to suggest we need to take all human judgement out of personal safety (for all the reasons previously mentioned in this article), but we need to make sure that safety, induction, signage, OH&S policies and leadership interventions are all designed to trigger desired behaviour.

Bias 3: Loss aversion and status quo bias

People want to maintain the status quo in order to avoid responsibility and exposure to criticism or risk. People have a desire to stay the same and are generally averse to change. The reason for this is that potential losses are weighed more heavily than potential gains. For instance, if you had $50 taken from you, the pain you would experience would be greater than the pleasure you would get from being given $50. In fact, in a game where you had a 50% chance of winning or losing, people will on average only play if the potential gain is three times greater than the potential loss. In our $50 example, the gain would have to be $150 for someone to risk losing $50. When it is an equal loss or gain scenario the odds have to be 90% in favour of a win for people to play.

Interestingly, this effect is reversed if somebody has already experienced a loss. So if someone in the previous game has lost $50, they are likely to play another game where the odds are staked at 90% in favour of a loss in order to have a 10% chance of regaining their $50. The pleasure gained from reclaiming the lost $50 is much greater than the pain that will be suffered from losing a further $50.

This effect can be seen in organisations, where change is seen as much riskier than maintaining the status quo. In this scenario they will tend to not adequately recognise the need for change on the basis that things are going well at the moment and should in all likelihood remain that way (note the availability heuristic). It is usually only when an accident occurs that processes will change, and in this environment of loss, the tendency to favour a more extreme or risky action in order to recuperate losses is very likely, making the situation even worse.

Organisations need to be able to recognise the need to change their rules-based safety culture to a principles-based safety mindset ahead of time, and prepare and plan for change appropriately to effectively improve the health and safety outcomes for all employees.

The impact of functional fit and cognitive bias

In the context of OH&S, an awareness of these biases is critical. As an employee, your own personal bias can cloud your ability to accurately assess dangerous situations. As a policy-maker, it can

Figure 3 - Organisational OH&S matrix

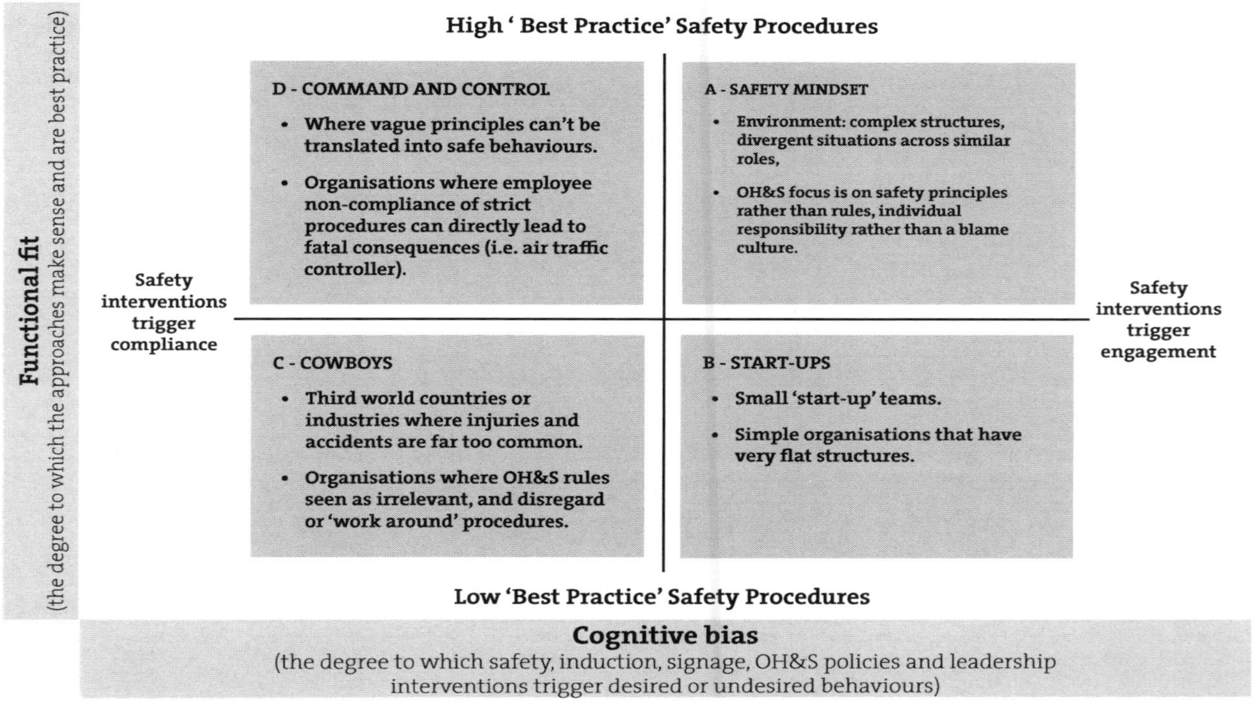

Functional fit
(the degree to which the approaches make sense and are best practice)

Safety interventions trigger compliance

High ' Best Practice' Safety Procedures

D - COMMAND AND CONTROL

- Where vague principles can't be translated into safe behaviours.
- Organisations where employee non-compliance of strict procedures can directly lead to fatal consequences (i.e. air traffic controller).

A - SAFETY MINDSET

- Environment: complex structures, divergent situations across similar roles.
- OH&S focus is on safety principles rather than rules, individual responsibility rather than a blame culture.

C - COWBOYS

- Third world countries or industries where injuries and accidents are far too common.
- Organisations where OH&S rules seen as irrelevant, and disregard or 'work around' procedures.

B - START-UPS

- Small 'start-up' teams.
- Simple organisations that have very flat structures.

Low 'Best Practice' Safety Procedures

Safety interventions trigger engagement

Cognitive bias
(the degree to which safety, induction, signage, OH&S policies and leadership interventions trigger desired or undesired behaviours)

cloud your ability to determine appropriate OH&S systems, and implement them in a way that will be understood and accepted by employees.

Figure 3 (opposite) outlines, at a high level, what leaders can do to adapt their processes in order to create safer environments by applying these two axes of performance.

A final thought on Occupational Health and Safety

1. Assess your company's level of complexity and maturity to indicate what the functional 'best practice' fit for OH&S processes is.

2. Align company OH&S practices and procedures to the needs of the organisation - 'functional fit'.

3. Identify cognitive biases at an individual and policy level, and make sure that these are not negatively impacting safe behaviours and policy.

4. Actively manage the impacts of cognitive bias on the culture of safety through active feedback loops and testing of assumptions.

The behavioural economics lens calls for large companies to fundamentally shift from a compliance-based systems approach (which gives control and responsibility to the systems) on the manager to a safety mindset (which shifts the focus to a far more distributed responsibility for safety).

It suggests that large and complex organisations should start to remove the concept of rules and regulations, and the total reliance on imperfect systems and the eradication of 'human' error, and migrate to a mindset based around safety principles to be embedded as business-as-usual. With this shift comes a change in culture from one of blame, to a shared responsibility for safety. In this way, OH&S policy becomes less about compliance and more about problem-solving, less about box-ticking and risk mitigation and more about awareness of the safety of yourself and those around you.

References and further reading

Battmann, W., & Klumb, P. (1991, January). *Behavioral Economics and Safety. In SPE Health Safety and Environment in Oil and Gas Exploration and Production Conference.* Society of Petroleum Engineers.

Burow, P (2013). *Core Beliefs. Harnessing the Power.* NeuroPower.

Burow, P. (2013). *NeuroPower. Leading with Neuro Intelligence (Third Ed.).* Copernicus Publishing Pty Ltd.

Dekker, S. (2014). *The Field Guide to Understanding 'Human Error'.* Ashgate Publishing, Ltd.

Dekker, S (2013). *Resilience. Online video published on May 29, 2013* Retrieved from: https://www.youtube.com/watch?v=o3L_TQG-xBs&index=1&list=PLMGi4vxpbgBEkA3-zC5DwoidPblsFbAsE

Dekker, S. (2003). *Failure to adapt or adaptations that fail: contrasting models on procedures and safety.* Applied ergonomics, 34(3), 233-238.

Gino, F., & Pisano, G. P. (2011). Why leaders don't learn from success. Harvard Business Review, 89(4), 68-74.

Kahneman, Daniel. (2011). *Thinking, Fast and Slow*: Macmillan.

Kahneman, D, & Tversky, A. (1979). *Prospect Theory: An analysis of decision under risk.* Econometrica: Journal of the Econometric Society, 263-291.

Lloyds of London. Past performance is not an indicator of future returns, but is a significant factor for investors (press release). Halifax. retrieved from, http://www.lloydsbankinggroup. com/globalassets/documents/media/press-releases/ halifax/2013/1406_hsdl_markettracker.pdf

Reason, J., Parker, D., & Lawton, R. (1998). *Organizational controls and safety: The varieties of rule-related behaviour. Journal of occupational and organizational psychology,* 71(4), 289-304.

Chapter 6: When Good Teams Make Bad Decisions

by Peter Burow

Complex strategic decisions involving judgement, interpretation and complex trade-offs are at the centre of effective teamwork at senior levels of organisations. Yet leadership teams find it difficult to get it right. Perhaps this is because our brains have developed problem-solving processes that rely heavily on past experiences which significantly bias today's preferences.

In a study conducted by McKinsey of more than 1000 major investments, it emerged that when leadership teams understand how to mediate their biases in decision-making they achieved returns of up to seven percentage points higher. (For more on this study, see The Case for Behavioral Strategy, McKinsey Quarterly, March 2010.) Cognitive bias is real and alive in most leadership teams. In this article I will outline the top 20 decision-making biases that derail executive teams, how to detect which of these most impact your team and how to minimise their effect.

How cognitive bias and group-think undermine judgement

We all like to think that we make decisions logically and objectively. Neuroscientists working with economists are discovering, however, that our decision-making isn't as rational as we believe. In fact, the way our brains function means that we all have blind spots and biases that influence the choices we make. By learning how to spot the most common blind spots, both in yourself and in your team you can increase the effectiveness of your decisions.

Decision-making is one of the most important responsibilities of a leadership team. It's also often the hardest and riskiest part of the job. Poor decisions can damage the business and careers - sometimes permanently. Take the recent example of the Deepwater Horizon oil spill crisis in the US; bad luck or bad decision-making?

Of course it will be some time before the situation is fully analysed and properly understood, so any discussion is necessarily limited to theory or conjecture. But it's certainly an interesting case. From one perspective, it could be argued that BP CEO Tony Hayward presided over an organisational culture that permitted risk-taking, ignored expert advice, disregarded warnings about safety issues and hid facts. What if BP's failure to respond to the disaster itself with sufficient speed and attention was also a direct consequence of this flawed culture?

Tony Hayward's comments throughout the process are revealing: Hayward's apparent inability to understand public reaction to his comments makes him appear at best, defensive and out of touch with the reality of the situation and, at worst, weak, petty and selfish. But how could someone so senior with a team of top advisors be so blind? To find out, we need to look at the role blind spots play in how decisions are made.

The way our brain works can sabotage our decisions

As leaders, we are constantly called upon to deal with complexity. Faced with the need to process vast amounts of information in order to make decisions, we resort to unconscious routines. These mental shortcuts (also known as heuristics, or decision rules which are simple for the brain to compute) enable us to make decisions and avoid both 'information overload' and 'analysis-paralysis'. In general, heuristics are very useful when making most routine decisions or when time is of the essence, but they can also lead to severe and systematic errors in judgement.

Researchers at INSEAD, Harvard, Oxford and Stanford Universities have identified a whole series of such flaws in the way we think when making decisions (besides heuristics, others include 'motivational factors' and 'social influence'). Of course, what makes these blind spots so dangerous is their invisibility. Because they are biases that are hardwired into our brains, we fail to recognise them and repeatedly make the same mistakes. These blind spots effectively create holes in our reasoning ability which, over time, produces recurring patterns of erroneous decision-making. In a group, the combined, overlapping biases of the individuals in the team reinforce and amplify biases. This can result in disastrous decisions.

While no one can entirely rid their mind of these ingrained patterns, it is possible to learn strategies to compensate for bias. The best approach is always awareness and the first step is to understand how these blind spots are formed. Executives who familiarise themselves with these blind spots and the diverse forms they take can consciously adapt their decision-making processes to ensure that the decisions they make are sound.

How emotions colour our thinking - our core beliefs at work

While neuroscientists continue to grapple with the complex ways that emotions interact with and influence the cognitive skills involved in decision-making, one thing is clear: emotions play a crucial role. In fact, we actually can't make decisions without them. By informing our desires, preferences and aversions, emotions shape our rational calculations. This is useful and

Over the course of our lives, each of us has developed a complex matrix of core beliefs that we believe will keep us 'safe' in the world.

necessary, because if we didn't have an emotional response to something (one way or another) we wouldn't be motivated to make a decision about it. Complete apathy leads to total lack of interest – we 'tune out'.

Problems develop, however, because our emotional responses inform our rational decision-making in a way that perpetuates our own personal philosophy on life (our unique worldview). Neuroeconomics describes people who decide different things in identical situations as different 'types'. These types are described as having different decision rules or different core beliefs.

Core beliefs are deep-seated perceptions that everyone has about the world around them. Over the course of our lives, each of us has developed a complex matrix of core beliefs that we believe will keep us 'safe' in the world. These beliefs have evolved over millennia to help us respond quickly and unthinkingly to dangerous situations; they act as our survival strategies and are embedded in the most primitive parts of our brain.

System 1 and System 2 - your emotional and rational brain

The interaction of our emotion-based core beliefs and our rational brain is illustrated in Diagram 1 - 'How the Brain Makes Decisions'. It shows how the two cognitive systems in our brain interact to make decisions and ultimately produce behaviour.

As Daniel Kahneman (who won a Nobel prize for his work in the area of neuroeconomics) explains, these two systems differ in speed, flexibility and operation.

The operations of System 1 (our emotional and most primitive brain – where our core beliefs live) are typically fast, automatic, effortless, associative, implicit (not available to introspection) and often emotionally charged; they are also governed by habit and therefore difficult to control or modify. The operations of

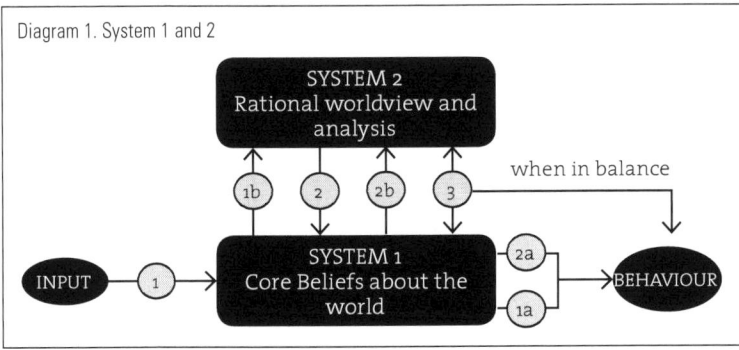

Diagram 1. System 1 and 2

System 2 (our rational, more evolved and modern brain) are slower, serial, effortful, more likely to be consciously monitored and deliberately controlled; they are also relatively flexible.

Both Systems 1 and 2 influence our judgements and choices - meaning that how we feel about something is as important as what our reasoning tells us about it. While this may conflict with our view of our own decision-making as highly rational, it often lines up with our experience of other people (who we see as occasionally irrational and emotional when we are arguing with them).

What makes this process particularly hard to track in ourselves is our tendency to rely on our primitive brain with its relatively simple (emotionally-charged core belief) evaluations to arrive at our decisions. We do this because it's so much easier and requires far less effort than using our rational brain. We then retrospectively justify (or post-rationalise) our core belief-based decisions using our rational brain and see them as rational choices.

In this way, each core belief's survival strategy filters out important data. This produces blind spots in System 1's emotional responses that influence what otherwise seem to be System 2's rational decisions. They are therefore linked to the many forms of what psychologists call 'cognitive bias', which is a tendency to draw incorrect conclusions in certain circumstances based on partial evidence.

An understanding of your own core beliefs is a great asset for any current or aspiring leader because it enables you to predict and therefore circumvent likely cognitive biases, thereby increasing the effectiveness of your decision-making.

In the same way, insights about core beliefs and how they drive our decision-making can also be applied in a team context; by understanding the core belief profiles of the team, it becomes

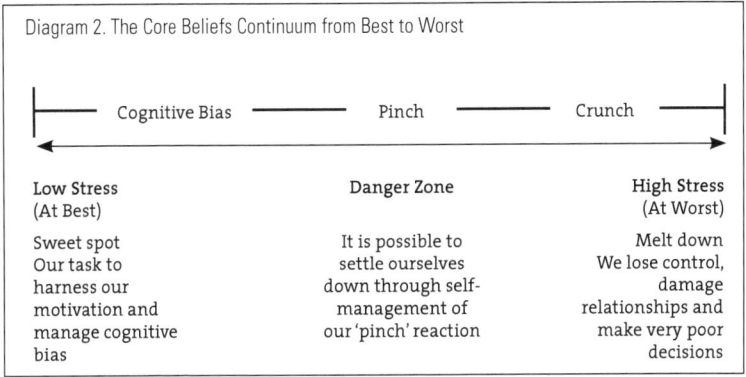

Diagram 2. The Core Beliefs Continuum from Best to Worst

Cognitive Bias	Pinch	Crunch
Low Stress (At Best)	**Danger Zone**	**High Stress** (At Worst)
Sweet spot Our task to harness our motivation and manage cognitive bias	It is possible to settle ourselves down through self-management of our 'pinch' reaction	Melt down We lose control, damage relationships and make very poor decisions

possible to predict the most likely accumulative and amplified cognitive biases that the team will experience in group decision-making processes.

Furthermore, because emotion is so central to our decision-making, the impact of our core belief-driven survival strategies vary according to our level of stress (see Diagram 2).

At best, when everything is proceeding as 'business-as-usual' and we are experiencing healthy levels of stress, our core beliefs help us make timely decisions. While these decisions may be correct, they are inherently biased. With awareness, we can learn to manage these biases using our rational brain.

As we become slightly stressed, our core beliefs encode the sorts of things that are likely to trigger us emotionally (based on whatever it is that we learnt to associate with survival when we were young). As the stress intensifies, we can get to an emotional tipping point, when we get triggered because we subjectively perceive (usually inaccurately) that our survival is being threatened. This explains why you might find some thing frustrating, annoying or infuriating, while others seem blissfully unaware it even happened - you simply have different core belief survival strategies that are wired to see different things as potential threats.

Table 1. The Nine Core Belief Types

The Nine Core Belief Types
Each of us has three of these core beliefs:

Core Belief Profile 1 – Perfectionists | Focus: Integrity/Clarity
Driven by the belief that you must be good and right to be worthy.
Consequently, are conscientious, responsible, improvement-oriented and
self-controlled, but also can be critical, resentful and self-judging.

Core Belief Profile 2 – Helpers | Focus: Influence
Driven by the belief that you must give fully to others to be loved.
Consequently, are caring, helpful, supportive and relationship-oriented, but
also can be prideful, overly intrusive and demanding.

Core Belief Profile 3 – Achievers | Focus: Achieving Results
Driven by the belief that you must accomplish and succeed to be loved.
Consequently, are industrious, fast-paced, goal-focused and efficiency-
oriented, but also can be inattentive to feelings, impatient and image-driven.

Core Belief Profile 4 – Artists | Focus: Elite Standards
Driven by the belief that you must obtain the longed-for ideal relationship or
situation to be loved. Consequently, are idealistic, deeply feeling, empathetic
and authentic to self, but also dramatic, moody and sometimes self-absorbed.

Core Belief Profile 5 – Analysts | Focus: Analysis/Depth of Technical Knowledge
Driven by the belief that you must protect yourself from a world that
demands too much and gives too little to assure life. Consequently, are self-
sufficiency seeking, non-demanding, analytical/thoughtful and unobtrusive,
but also can be withholding, detached and overly private.

Core Belief Profile 6 – Loyal Sceptics | Focus: Loyalty/Scepticism
Driven by the belief that you must gain protection and security in a
hazardous world you just can't trust. Consequently, are themselves
trustworthy, inquisitive, good friends and questioning, but also can be overly
doubtful, accusatory and fearful.

Core Belief Profile 7 – Epicures | Focus: New Opportunities
Driven by the belief that you must keep life up and open to assure a good life.
Consequently, are optimistic, upbeat, possibility- and pleasure-seeking and
adventurous, but also can be pain-avoidant, uncommitted and self-serving.

Core Belief Profile 8 – The Boss | Focus: All or Nothing
Driven by the belief that you must be strong and powerful to assure
protection and regard in a tough world. Consequently, are justice-seeking,
direct, strong and action-oriented, but also overly impactful, excessive and
sometimes impulsive.

Core Belief Profile 9 – Peacemakers | Focus: Minimising Conflict
Driven by the belief that to be loved and valued you must blend in and go
along to get along. Consequently, are self-forgetting, harmony-seeking,
comfortable and steady, but also conflict avoidant and sometimes stubborn.

When something triggers you emotionally, you reach this emotional tipping point. This is also known as experiencing an emotional 'pinch'. Unfortunately, as your stress levels increase further, usually because the issue isn't addressed, the pinch can progress further to a second, much more dramatic tipping point called a 'crunch'. This highly emotional state often causes damage to relationships, both personal and professional, and leads to very poor decisions.

The rest of this article will be focusing on the cognitive bias aspect of this continuum rather than the pinch or crunch tipping points. While it assumes at least a basic understanding of the Core Belief Profiles in making the links to different cognitive biases, that's certainly not necessary to grasp the key concepts we'll be discussing. As an introduction, Table 1 provides a brief overview of the nine Core Belief types. If you're interested, you can find out more information about the Core Beliefs – and start the process of identifying your own and those of your team – by reading the book, Core Beliefs: Harnessing the Power (Burow, 2010).

Understanding cognitive bias

Researchers agree there are at least twenty distinct cognitive biases that can be tracked and measured both in individuals and collectively in teams. This does not include biases caused by an inability to understand and work with numbers - also known as innumeracy biases (see Table 1). The balance of the biases can be grouped into five main categories:

1. **Pattern recognition biases:** Misinterpreting conceptual relationships or identifying patterns where there are none;

2. **Action-orientated biases:** The drive to take action too quickly;

3. **Stability biases:** The tendency toward inertia in the presence of uncertainty;

4. **Interest biases**: Arising in the presence of conflicting incentives (including non-monetary and even purely emotional ones);

5. **Social biases**: The preference for harmony over conflict.

Cognitive bias in action: poor decision-making at BP

Returning to the BP situation, the initial information available suggests that there were the apparent elements of underestimating risk, ignoring advice, disregarding warnings about safety issues and post-rationalising. These are all classic markers of Confirmation Bias.

This suggests that BP's decision-making may have been biased towards confirming existing beliefs by seeking only information that confirmed preconceptions and by ignoring evidence in support of other viewpoints. Unchecked, Confirmation Bias results in ill-informed, narrow and partial decisions most commonly seen in situations of 'Groupthink'.

Groups with this bias often exhibit a degree of 'we're right, you're wrong' certainty that is often unwarranted. In the BP case, this may help explain the wildly inaccurate early estimates regarding the environmental impact of the disaster.

BP's actions also showed signs of three other biases: Unfounded Optimism Bias (being excessively optimistic about the future and unrealistic about the likelihood of positive/negative events), Overconfidence Bias (overestimating their ability to affect future outcomes in the cleanup process) and False Consensus Bias (overestimating the extent to which others shared BP's perspective on the disaster and instead assuming that everyone else thinks the same way they do).

Each of these biases is common to the Core Belief Profile 3. Perhaps the team had too many Core Belief Profile 3s in its composition,

Table 2. How core beliefs lead to individual cognitive bias in decision-making

CATEGORY OF BIASES	COGNITIVE BIAS	CORE BELIEF PROFILE								
		1	2	3	4	5	6	7	8	9
PATTERN RECOGNITION BIASES	Saliency Bias: Giving disproportionate weight to recent dramatic events, thereby exaggerating the probability of rare but catastrophic occurrences	✓	✓		✓		✓			✓
	Confirmation Bias: Seeking information that confirms an existing perspective and ignoring evidence that supports alternative views	✓	✓	✓	✓	✓	✓	✓	✓	✓
	False Analogies Bias: Relying on comparisons with situations that are not directly comparable	✓	✓	✓		✓				
	Champion Bias: Evaluating options on the basis of the track record of the individual who suggests it rather than on the facts	✓	✓					✓	✓	
	Availability Bias: Overestimating the risks of an event that can be imagined vividly, while leaving oneself exposed to less vivid risks		✓		✓		✓		✓	
ACTION-ORIENTED BIASES	Overconfidence Bias: Overestimating one's ability to affect future outcomes, taking credit for past outcomes and minimising the role of chance. Also overestimating our skill level relative to others				✓			✓	✓	
	Unfounded Optimism Bias: Being excessively optimistic about the future and unrealistic about the likelihood of positive/negative events				✓			✓	✓	
	Competitor Neglect Bias: Planning without factoring in competitive responses	✓			✓	✓				✓
	Overcautiousness Bias: Focusing on worst case analysis and failing to take any appropriate action at all (i.e. the 'Prudence Trap')	✓	✓		✓	✓	✓			✓
	All or Nothing Bias: Failing to take a portfolio risk and instead seeking complete protection (i.e. putting all the eggs in one basket and then watching the basket)	✓			✓			✓	✓	
STABILITY BIASES	Status Quo Bias: Favouring options that perpetuate the status quo (to avoid both taking action/responsibility and opening oneself to criticism/risk)	✓	✓		✓	✓	✓			
	Sunk Costs Bias: Making choices that justify past flawed decisions, thereby avoiding acknowledging a past error	✓			✓	✓			✓	✓
	Anchoring Bias: Giving disproportionate weight to the first information received		✓	✓				✓	✓	
	Loss Aversion Bias: Being swayed by the framing rather than the facts themselves (i.e. being risk-averse when an option is posed in terms of making gains and risk-seeking when framed in terms of avoiding losses)	✓	✓		✓	✓	✓			✓
INTEREST BIASES	Misaligned Perception Bias: Choosing options that align with one's individual perception of the hierarchy or relative weight of goals pursued by the organisation (rather than on an agreed understanding of the hierarchy/weight)				✓	✓		✓	✓	
	Inappropriate Attachment Bias: Preferring options that support or are linked to one's emotional attachment to certain individuals or elements of the business		✓	✓			✓	✓	✓	✓
SOCIAL BIASES	Herding Instinct Bias: Conforming to the dominant views of the group	✓	✓	✓						✓
	Sunflower Management Bias: Aligning with the views of the leader or ultimate decision-maker (whether expressed or assumed)	✓	✓	✓			✓			✓
	False Consensus Bias: Overestimating the extent to which others share our views, beliefs and experiences	✓						✓	✓	
	Default Bias: Defaulting to an existing strong social norm	✓	✓	✓		✓	✓			✓

or perhaps they had a number of Core Belief Profile 3 advisors. Or the BP culture may reflect the legacies of Core Belief Profile 3s in the past.

While we can hypothesise about the decision-making factors that contributed to the accident, it's important to note that BP is not alone in experiencing biased decision-making.

When we work with Australian leadership teams and boards that are facing highly stressful situations (e.g. shareholder outrage at poor performance), they can often track back the seeds of the situation they are facing to a long line of poor decisions that reflect the primary biases of the team. Unchecked, cognitive bias leads to poor commercial performance, because the crucial decisions from the top are flawed.

Awareness is the key to counteracting bias and overcoming decision-making blind spots

Highly complex and important decisions are the most prone to distortion by cognitive bias because they tend to involve the most assumptions, the most estimates, and the most inputs from the greatest number of people. And, of course, the higher the stakes, the higher the risk of falling prey to one or more psychological biases because we are stressed and by nature therefore more emotional.

Even if teams can't eradicate the distortions ingrained in the way their members' minds work, they can build tests and discipline into their decision-making process that can uncover errors in thinking before they become errors in judgement and lead to disastrous decisions.

Cognitively balancing cognitive bias

In a team context, the most effective way to minimise the impact of cognitive bias on group decisions is to create awareness of the team's bias and to use key questions to balance the bias. When I work with leadership teams, we enhance and sharpen the focus of this awareness by identifying the exact Core Belief Profiles in the team using a tool called the Core Beliefs Inventory and then cross tabulate this with the 20 biases (see Table 2). With this information, it is possible to tally which of the twenty cognitive biases will have the greatest influence over the team. The questions outlined in Table 3 can be used to counteract the team's biases and drive more effective decision-making. Calculate key high priority biases within your team and then workshop the relevant questions.

Decision-making, either as a leader or as part of a team, is never an easy process. Unfortunately, as the stakes increase, so too does the likelihood that the outcome will be driven by cognitive bias, rather than the reality of the situation. The good news is that with awareness and questioning, you can significantly reduce cognitive bias. And, once done, the effectiveness of your decisions will increase – to the benefit of both you and your team.

Checklist for countering your team's decision-making bias

- Use the Core Beliefs Inventory to identify the Core Belief Profiles of your team members.
- Use Table 2 to calculate the highest cognitive biases in the team.
- Use questions that balance up the cognitive biases (sample questions in Table 3) to shape decision-making.
- Monitor team meetings to ensure you maintain the rage against faulty decision-making caused by cognitive bias.

Table 3. Sample questions to counteract cognitive bias

	Cognitive Bias	Questions for bringing the bias into consciousness
Pattern Recognition Biases	Saliency Bias	If we knew for certain that everything would go smoothly over the next 12 months, and that no rare but catastrophic events are about to occur, what might you decide to do differently?
	Confirmation Bias	What information can you find that does not support the current way of thinking?
	False Analogies Bias	What differences can you find between the current challenge and the past situations that have been referenced in the decision-making process? List as many differences as possible.
	Champion Bias	If this option were being proposed by an unknown person from outside the team, how would you objectively assess its merits?
	Availability Bias	If you knew that none of the major risks you've already identified would eventuate, would that change your decision? What additional unlikely risks can you think of?
Action-oriented Biases	Overconfidence Bias	Assuming you have little ability to control all future outcomes, what role would you say chance could play in future success?
	Unfounded Optimism Bias	If you were to look at this situation from a pessimistic viewpoint, what might you see that could go wrong?
	Competitor Neglect Bias	How are your competitors likely to respond to the implementation of your plan? How might that affect its efficacy?
	Overcautious-ness Bias	What is the best case scenario in terms of outcome? For that situation to eventuate, what would you need to do now?
	All or Nothing Bias	How else could you apply at least some of your resources across a number of portfolios?
Stability Biases	Status Quo Bias	How could we approach this issue in a completely new way? What benefits would this bring?
	Sunk Costs Bias	If you were an external expert, and knew nothing about the history of this issue to date, what would you recommend? If there were no financial issues to consider (i.e. the financial slate were wiped clean) what approach would you adopt?
	Anchoring Bias	How many different sources of information have been considered on this issue? How many experts have been consulted? What was the trend of the last batch of information received? What did the information suggest on balance?
	Loss Aversion Bias	What losses could be avoided by adopting this approach?
Interest Biases	Misaligned Perception Bias	Which of the organisation's goals does this approach further? Would everyone agree that this is a high priority?
	Inappropriate Attachment Bias	If this decision were about a different part of the business/involved different people, how might your approach be different?

Cognitive Bias	Questions for bringing the bias into consciousness
Social Biases	
Herding Instinct Bias	If this were a decision that was solely your responsibility and for which you alone would be held accountable, what would you do?
Sunflower Management Bias	If you could just take this decision yourself rather than aligning with the leader, what would your recommendation be?
False Consensus Bias	How are the drivers of the different stakeholders different from our drivers? What stakeholders will be disadvantaged by this decision and why? What would need to happen for the key stakeholder groups to consider the decision outstanding?
Default Bias	If a team at one of your major competitors was faced with this challenge, what would they do?

Chapter 7: Switching on Your Leadership Mindset

by Peter Burow and Anna Byrne

Neuroscience tells us when you learn how to switch into a constructive mindset, innovation and success follow. Fail to make this switch and the role of a leader becomes at best a discipline, and at worst an overwhelming responsibility that erodes resilience, creativity and quality of life.

Mastering the switch from an unconstructive to a constructive mindset is absolutely critical to performance and sustainability as a leader.

Reactive habitual and rational reasoning systems

Most of us are familiar with the fact that there are different systems within the human brain that control thinking and behaviour. While many of the 1970s generalisations about the 'left brain' and 'right brain' function that have crept into popular belief have more recently proved to be a fallacy, recent neuroscientific findings show there are two distinct and opposing systems in the brain that underlie the complex reasoning process.

In his 2011 book, *Thinking, Fast and Slow*, renowned Israeli-American psychologist Dr Daniel Kahneman identifies the emotional System 1 as the fast and intuitive system and the rational System 2 as the slower and deliberate system of reasoning.

Affective vs. cognitive, automatic vs. controlled and reactive vs. responsive are all labels that psychologists and researchers have used for these cognitive types since Schneider and Shiffrin's research in the 1970s, but we will refer to the terms 'emotional' and 'rational'.

The *emotional system* is focused on instinctive, automatic and habitual behaviour; or doing what comes naturally. It is rooted in the primitive survival system that was essential in the face of physical threat in the past; essentially it is fast and reactive, but unsophisticated and habitual. People often fail to recognise that their behaviour or decision-making has been affected by their emotional system.

The rational system is considered a more modern function of the brain, focused on dealing with high-level complexity and creating novel ideas and solutions. It is more pro-active and constructive than the emotional system and allows abstract, reflective and hypothetical thought processes. Most people have a good understanding of their rational system and, when asked about how they arrived at a particular decision (such as buying a house) they can usually recall their thought processes.

Professor Jonathan Evans, in his 2011 paper on dual process theories, points to the complexity of the issue though, noting that the application of this two-system theory to cognitive reasoning is no simple task.

He explains:

We do not move from Type 1 [emotional] to Type 2 [rational] thinking. Rather Type 1 thinking both competes with and shapes Type 2 thinking in adults. In fact, the literature on human reasoning suggests that intuitive and contextualised forms of thought are the most typical and commonplace in adult reasoning. However, abstract and hypothetical forms of thought are a distinctive feature of human intelligence that has allowed us to outperform all other species by a distance when it comes to novel thinking, problem-solving, design and consequential decision-making. Both of these types of thinking develop throughout childhood as well as the mechanisms that allow one or the other to take control of our behaviour as suits the situation. Understanding how this happens provides an essential challenge for theorists of cognitive development to meet.[1]

What are the ramifications of this for an organisation that relies on the ability of its leaders to think strategically and creatively, and to make highly effective decisions to drive performance?

How can organisations pivot to adopt better leadership strategies based around an enhanced understanding of human behaviour? How can leaders and their teams effectively learn to switch between systems situationally and automatically to achieve better results?

Happiness, positive psychology and human flourishing

Increasing time spent in the constructive mindset leads to considerable psychological and physiological benefits. The pursuit of happiness for people is more likely to be found when living in the creative, adaptable and constructive (positive) mindset.

Dr Martin Seligman notes that although a constructive mindset may not be natural from an evolutionary perspective, modern times dictate the adoption of a new positive psychology will provide mental and physical health benefits. He discusses how the stress and distress mindsets that were once necessary for survival, must move towards mindsets that encourage

---

1   The reactive habitual system within the brain corresponds closely to NeuroPower's Core Belief framework; and the rational system corresponds closely to NeuroPower's Strategic Mindset framework. NeuroPower has been applying these techniques to build team, leadership and organisational excellence in businesses in Australia and all over the world for decades.

communities to flourish, rather than just endure.

The power of positive emotions has also been said to 'broaden people's momentary thought-action repertoires, which in turn serves to build their enduring personal resources, ranging from physical and intellectual resources to social and psychological resources'. This is clearly the 'flourishing' of individuals, relationships, teams and organisations that Seligman refers to. Fredrickson and Losada define it further: "To flourish means to live within an optimal range of functioning, one that connotes goodness, generativity, growth, and resilience."

In their study of happiness, Lyubomirsky et al. identify three main factors that affect happiness: genetics, circumstantial factors and self-determined activities/practices. Of these, the one we have most control over is the last factor. They go on to identify the ways to increase happiness as the following: choosing appropriate activities, applying effort to start the activity and to see it through, and then in making it habitual.

Generally, we are the sum of our habits; but there is an apparent dichotomy at play here, as Lyubomirsky et al. point out: "Is it not the case that acquiring a habit means that one has turned a formerly conscious activity into an unconscious routine, practiced automatically and without variation? If so, the individual will experience hedonic adaptation to that activity, such that it loses its happiness-boosting potential."

Their solution to this is found in adopting a mindful implementation of the activity in question through, "optimal timing and variety in the ways they practice an activity." We will look more at forming habits later.

Implications for leadership

If we accept that it is desirable to develop a constructive mindset, both for individuals' well-being and growth, and, by extension, for enhanced organisational performance, how do leaders model and embed this?

It requires leaders with the necessary commitment and patience, as well as psychological and behavioural understanding, to drive a new culture. Team members will need to be encouraged to adopt the more challenging, but more constructive, rational mindset, as opposed to the 'fallback' emotional thinking that at first seems an easier pathway.

Given the challenges and disruptions of the average person's work day, is it unreasonable to assume that leaders can always remain in a constructive mindset? As situations and issues arise, the brain's fallback mechanism naturally switches back into a reactive, survival state. When we receive bad news about a key project, the brain's natural response is emotional (unconstructive) rather than rational (constructive).

However, with the right techniques it is possible to master this reaction. In fact, leadership research shows that it is one of the founding skills of any good leader and great leaders help team members to do likewise.

Leaders first need to understand and recognise their own triggers; then they must practice making the SWITCH when they sense these triggers being activated.

Ultimately, they need to create an environment where teams are able and comfortable to follow suit. Once people see the positive results from their leaders, where reaction is converted into resolution, they naturally want to follow.

The ability to SWITCH should be treated as a learned skill, where the more it is practiced, the more it becomes embedded as second nature. The brain effectively forms new neural pathways to increase our ability to switch, and this allows us to proactively move our constructive mindset from 'state' to 'trait'.

Positive intelligence-boosting habits

In his recent book, *Positive Intelligence*, Shirzad Chamine considers, "why only 20% of teams and individuals achieve their true potential." He notes that almost all executives in his lectures suffer from 'saboteurs' that cause 'significant harm' to their achievement. These saboteurs are in the mind and, therefore, ultimately under our control.

Chamine recommends a series of techniques for overcoming this, and to develop the habit of remaining in the positive and constructive mindset, and to boost what he calls positive intelligence (PQ).

Some of these habit-forming techniques include:

- Commanding yourself to stop being lost in thought and instead become aware of your physical sensations. This exercise activates the medial prefrontal cortex (mPFC), which is the same region that enables us to switch to the constructive mindset. When performed frequently enough, this helps to permanently create new neural pathways that remain active even when the person is no longer focused on the exercise.

- Another way of stimulating the mPFC is to focus for 10 seconds on your physical sensations (any one of the five senses) when performing routine daily tasks, like brushing teeth, exercising and eating. Smelling the toothpaste, listening to your breathing or focusing on tasting food will help you let go of thoughts and make the switch.

- Practice these techniques every time you perform a particular daily routine; when you observe yourself falling victim to your mental 'saboteurs' (like anxiety, anger or sadness) take energy away from the saboteur and switch it on your positive intelligence. Soon you will find yourself able to recognise and reverse the effects of the 'saboteur'.

In his 2002 book, *The New Psycho-Cybernetic*, Dr Maxwell Maltz postulates that it takes 21 days for the necessary neural pathways to form and replace the old ones, in order for new habits to be created. Three weeks seems like a small price to pay for a paved gateway to a constructive, rational mindset.

'Switch' strategies for leadership

The goal is that when the leader senses reactionary behaviour, they are able to automatically re-enter the constructive mindset.

The nine Cs described by Stanford University Professor, Dr David Daniels, are also a helpful way to self-manage and keep yourself in a constructive leader mindset[2].

1. Center Yourself. Center yourself by practicing the breathing exercise for a few moments.

2. Cultivate Your Consciousness. Cultivate consciousness in yourself by using self- observation to discover what your current preoccupations are.

3. Collect Your Energy. Collect your energy back into yourself, into the gravitational center of your body, when it wants to discharge into habitual reactions.

4. Contain Your Energy. Contain your energy by concentrating your attention on experiencing your feelings instead of discharging your energy in a habitual, type-determined way. Resist the urge to take immediate action.

5. Consider the Meaning of Your Usual Reaction. Consider what your usual automatic response is about by using inner inquiry and self-reflection.

6. Convert Your Energy to Conscious Conduct. Convert your habitual responses into conscious conduct by using your awareness to coach and encourage yourself to try healthier courses of action.

2   What Chamine discusses is very similar to the techniques we use for teaching leaders in habitualising the SWITCH to the constructive mindset.

7. Compassion. Manifest compassion by adopting a kind and caring attitude toward yourself and others.

8. Consequences. Consider the consequences, or effects, of your conscious conduct by noticing the impact of your behaviour on yourself and on others.

9. Clarity. Gain clarity about the process of personal and professional development by reflecting upon and internalizing the previous eight elements of development.

Summary

A constructive mindset enables individuals to most effectively process information, make decisions and lead teams. While external circumstances are often out of our influence, our mindset is always in our control. As humans, we are designed to automatically use our emotional system when there is a stressful situation needing a fast response. Accessing our rational system is less instinctive and uses more effort. It takes persistent practice to master the SWITCH from our emotional to our rational system, but the benefits outweigh the effort. If we master this SWITCH as leaders; we triumph in leadership, innovation and performance.

Switch # 1
Labelling

1 Pause and notice the emotion that is sitting in the background.

2 Acknowledge that you are masking an emotion.

3 Identify the emotion and label it.

4 Identify the trigger that may have caused the emotion.

When you mask your emotions, you limit your cognitive capacity. Use the labelling switch to free cognitive capacity for the task at hand.

© NEURO POWER PTY LTD 2014

Switch # 2
High Values

1 Recall your top three personal values that define your leadership style.

2 How would you respond to this situation in line with these values?

3 If you had to take the first step, what would it be?

Living in line with your values moves your motivation from obsessive to harmonious passion.

© NEURO POWER PTY LTD 2014

Switch # 3
Mentor

1 Recall one of your mentors.

2 How would your mentor respond to this situation? (Think, Feel, Act).

3 What would your mentor advise you to do?

Identifying with a role model/ mentor you respect will focus your attention on constructive problem-solving and reduce the chance you'll regret your actions later.

© NEURO POWER PTY LTD 2014

Switch # 4
Cognitive Focus

1 Choose your emotions rather than let them choose you.

2 Is this emotion helpful to you right now?

3 Consider putting your current emotion to one side and allocating time to 'solve' the issue triggering the emotion and in the meantime choosing another emotion for the short term that will help you achieve your goals.

Living in line with your values moves your motivation from obsessive to harmonious passion.

© NEURO POWER PTY LTD 2014

Switch # 5
Significance

1 Consider whether this will be an issue in 10 years.

2 What are the three most important things in your life/career at the moment?

When we are below the line, it's difficult to see issues with perspective, but doing so can help us move above the line.

© NEURO POWER PTY LTD 2014

Switch # 6
Talk

1 Choose a person who is a good non-judgemental listener and ask if they mind you 'venting'.

2 Once you have 'vented', shift to a solution-focused mindset.

3 How have you solved similar situations in the past?

4 How might this approach be adapted to the current situation?

When we are below the line, it's difficult to see issues with perspective, but doing so can help us move above the line.

© NEURO POWER PTY LTD 2014

Switch # 7
Photo

1 Select a photo of someone who always brings out the best in you.

2 Get it framed so it's suitable for your desk, or set it as a screen saver on your phone or tablet.

3 When you move below the line, look at the photo for 30 seconds.

4 Observe as your emotions shift from below to above the line.

Focusing on this person enables a positive mindset, which allows your brain to become rational and logical again.

© NEURO POWER PTY LTD 2014

Switch # 8
Music

1 Have a favourite song easily accessible on your phone and computer.

2 When you move below the line, listen to the song.

3 If you're still below the line, listen to it again or use another switch.

Music triggers areas in the brain that release dopamine, which enables you to release the negative pattern.

© NEURO POWER PTY LTD 2014

Switch # 9
Breathe

1 Focus only on your breathing.

2 Place your hand on your stomach and breathe deeply, allowing your stomach to expand while you inhale.

3 Repeat at least five times.

Deep breathing lowers your stress hormones by 30%, which has an instant physiological impact on your body.

© NEURO POWER PTY LTD 2014

Switch # 10
Five Senses

1 Through your five senses, focus on where you are right now for 30 seconds.

2 What can you see?
What can you hear?
What can you taste?
What can you touch?
What can you smell?

Focused attention has many benefits including increased immune system, better quality sleep and lower levels of depression and anxiety.

© NEURO POWER PTY LTD 2014

Switch # 11
Walk

1 Go for a walk.

2 Notice something you have never seen before: 'what's changed?'

3 Discipline yourself to think about what has caused the switch.

Walking releases the natural 'feel good' hormones called endorphins, instantly lifting your mood and allowing you to see the bigger picture.

© NEURO POWER PTY LTD 2014

References

Burow, P. (2005). *Personality and Performance.* Australia: Copernicus Publishing Pty Ltd.

Burow, P. (2010). *NeuroPower: Leading with NeuroIntelligence. Australia:* Copernicus Publishing Pty Ltd.

Evans, Jonathan St B.T. *Dual-process theories of reasoning: Contemporary issues and developmental applications.* Developmental Review 31 (2011) 86-102. Doi:10.1016/j. dr.2011.07.007

Fredrickson, Barbara L. T*he Role of Positive Emotions in Positive Psychology: The Broaden and Build Theory of Positive Emotions.* American Psychological Association (2001) Vol 56, No. 3, 218-226. Doi:10.1037/0003-066X.56.3.218

Fredrickson, Barbara L., Losada, Marcial F. Positive *Affect and the Complex Dynamics of Human Flourishing.* American Psychological Association (2005) Vol60, No. 7, 675-686. Doi:10.1037/0003-066X.60.7.678

Kahneman, D. (2011). *Thinking, Fast and Slow.* New York: Farrar, Straus and Giroux.

Lyubomirsky, S., Sheldon, K.M., Schkade, D. *Pursuing Happiness: The Architecture of Sustainable Change.* Educational Publishing Foundation (2005) Doi:10.1037/1089-2680.9.2.111

Seligman, M.P. Positive *Psychology: An Introduction.* American Psychological Association (2001) Vol 55, No. 1, 5-14. Doi:10.1037/0003-066X.55.1.5

Conclusion

The real gift that Daniel Kahneman and Amos Tversky gave us, with the development of behavioural economics, was a language and a framework with which to better understand our own decision-making processes. It gives us insight into the 'black-box' of our irrational judgements and increases our awareness of our cognitive bias leading to more rational decision-making.

As with most scientific research, there is a real skill in being able to translate scientific insights to our own lives and to improve the systems and practices of the world around us. Hopefully, this book has not only increased your own awareness of the cognitive biases that are present in your decision-making, but starts to show how to practically apply this new found awareness to improve organisational behaviour and workplace practices. The end goal is people, at all levels of society and cultures, can make better decisions for themselves and the people around them. For organisations, it is about understanding cognitive bias to improve the well-being of staff and increasing fair and ethical behaviour to customers and suppliers.

I encourage you all to discover the cognitive biases that underpin your judgements and decision-making. Increase your awareness of your biases in order to live a life of character and hardwire this character into your brain until it is transformed into wisdom. Together we can all make better decisions and create a better world.

About the Authors

Peter Burow is an expert in leadership and team development, transformational change and employee engagement. Peter is internationally regarded as a trusted advisor and expert facilitator of senior executive teams in driving individual, team and organisational performance. He has developed the ground-breaking NeuroPower framework - a system explaining human behaviour through the integration of neuroscience, psychology and best-practice management theory used by accredited practitioners in Australia, USA, Thailand, Malaysia, India and the UAE. He is the author of numerous books and is Executive Chairman of the NeuroPower Group.

Phil Slade is an expert in behavioural economics, psychology and political science, with a particular interest in applying insights from neuropsychology and behavioural economics to ethics, marketing, leadership and cultural development. Phil has organised and led large teams in the delivery of complex projects, and specialises in conflict management, team engagement, strategic planning and leadership coaching. Phil is also an award-winning orchestral composer for stage and screen and is author of numerous journal articles and hosts his own podcast on behavioural economics.

Misha Byrne is an awarded neuroscientist with a background in researching the brain mechanisms behind how we monitor and improve our own performance. He has extensive experience in the collection and analysis of research data in marketing, stakeholder engagement and cultural analysis with working as a researcher in Cognitive Neuroscience at the Queensland Brain Institute with a specific focus in quantitative behavioural genetics. Misha specialises in taking the latest insights from neuroscience and creating real-world business applications.

Zane Harris is a Human Resources professional with extensive experience managing organisational-wide change and learning and development programs. He specialises in applying the insights from neuroscience to significantly accelerate the development of teams in order to drive organisational performance and create cultural alignment within blue chip corporations, government departments and rapidly growing SMEs. He trains the NeuroPower framework with senior leaders in a range of organisations across Australia, South East Asia and the Middle East. He is the author of numerous articles and is CEO of the NeuroPower Group.

Anna Byrne has a background in law, political science and psychology with significant experience in the development, implementation and management of organisational change and transformation programs that solve complex problems, shift behaviour and drive employee engagement. She has a particular interest in applying behavioural strategies to develop initiatives that optimise engagement, accelerate the embedding of change and drive tangible change in the workplace. Anna specialises in coaching leaders and managers in transformational project management, employee engagement and strategic communications.

Printed in Great Britain
by Amazon.co.uk, Ltd.,
Marston Gate.